God is Real

God is Real

Roy Davidson

CREATION HOUSE
A STRANG COMPANY

GOD IS REAL by Roy Davidson
Published by Creation House
A Strang Company
600 Rinehart Road
Lake Mary, Florida 32746
www.creationhouse.com

This book or parts thereof may not be reproduced in any form, stored in a retrieval system, or transmitted in any form by any means—electronic, mechanical, photocopy, recording, or otherwise—without prior written permission of the publisher, except as provided by United States of America copyright law.

Scripture quotations are from the Holy Bible, New International Version of the Bible. Copyright © 1973, 1978, 1984, International Bible Society. Used by permission.

Cover design by Jerry Pomales

Copyright © 2008 by Roy Davidson
All rights reserved

Library of Congress Control Number: 2008929187
International Standard Book Number: 978-1-59979-396-2

08 09 10 11 12 — 9 8 7 6 5 4 3 2 1
Printed in the United States of America

DEDICATION

To my grandpa, Roy Hawkins, "Pop", 1897–1968

ACKNOWLEDGEMENT

With highest respect to John D. Eckrich M.D. from the Southwest Medical Group, St. Louis, Missouri, for allowing God to use him as a pillar of truth, faith, and healing.

CONTENTS

	Foreword xiii
	Preface xv
1.	A Nobody. 1
2.	*X* Means "Yes" 5
3.	Not Thirty, but Forty Feet 9
4.	Silence, Like in a Vacuum 17
5.	Bombarded 23
6.	Names Don't Matter 33
7.	I Guess So 43
8.	Sick and Tired 49
9.	Ghost vs. Spirit 61
10.	Blackout. 67
11.	Magic Money 71
12.	Who's There? 75
13.	Documented, Undeniable Proof 81
14.	Heavy Demons 89
15.	Unholy Yacht 103
16.	I'm a What? 109
17.	1994. 113

18.	No Mistakes	125
19.	Most Profound	133
20.	Guatemala	141
21.	Just Do It	151
22.	A God Thing	157
23.	Raise Your Hands	165
24.	Do It Yourself	175
25.	A Lot More	191
26.	Your Turn	197
	About the Author	201

FOREWORD

AFTER READING Roy's manuscript, I thought, "It has to be published." Some of the ministries he has done are amazing, especially considering that he is a husband, father, and layman, yet has traveled the world and impacted nations!

As a book, it has some shocking stories, several of them verging on the incredible, but the creditable stories give credibility to the incredible. We live in a world where people are hungry for the supernatural and many live by the direction of psychics, palm readers, astrologists, and the daily horoscope. Yet in the church, we are nervous or embarrassed by the supernatural power of God. Roy's book tells many super stories of God's power.

I believe people will enjoy reading the book and that many will be challenged to look for the supernatural power of God in their own lives.

Until all have heard,
—JACK HARRIS
President, Global Messenger Service

PREFACE

IF YOU'RE THE KIND OF PERSON WHO DOESN'T READ anything, much less books about miracles or spirituality, then you're a lot like me. It takes something pretty unique to get my attention. Well, I promise you, my testimonies will make you think.

The events are in chronological order as often as possible so you can see the transition in me and the increase of the supernatural in my life. Don't jump ahead to see where it's going or you won't understand what is happening. As my story unfolds, it will help you to consider the possibility of things you may not readily want to accept, but every story is true! In fact, most of the events recorded in this book were either witnessed by others or documented with evidence.

Now it's time to set the stage with who I am so I can tell you about the hard-to-believe, supernatural things. Here we go...

Chapter 1
A NOBODY

THERE ARE SO MANY UNEXPLAINABLE THINGS happening in the world today. I don't understand how people can ignore them and refuse to believe in supernatural events or miracles. Then you have people who believe something was a miracle, but they refuse to give the credit to God. In the back of their minds, they believe some coincidence or facts unknown to them must have been the real explanation. On top of that, there are people in church, at a wedding, or at a funeral praying to God, but they don't honestly believe God is real.

I know God is real. He has proven His existence to me. But why me? Who am I that God would do such unbelievable things for me? I'm a nobody. I've done lots of bad stuff. I'm as common as anyone else. There are plenty of other people who are much better persons than I am. To me, it seems they are much more deserving to have had some of the experiences I've had. And still, God chose to reveal Himself to me in ways that make other people envious.

Supernatural things may have already happened to you, and you may be letting yourself doubt that it really was God intervening in your life. If nothing supernatural has happened to you yet, God might bless you with a testimony of your own before you finish reading this book.

Anybody can have a great testimony—one much more profound than mine—but for one person to have as many as I have had, you might think I'm making them up. Now, what good would it do me to make them up? What reason or purpose would it serve me to make these things up? And why would I want to tell people preposterous stories and risk looking like a nut or a liar, unless they were true?

So again, why me? I've wondered this for the past five years. I know we are not supposed to question God, but I do. I figure I can get away with it if I pose my questions like I'm just pondering an issue and not really asking for an answer. For me, that has worked. I leave questions floating out there in a manner that says: "God, if I get an answer about this, great. And if I don't, OK; I guess I don't need to know yet." With that attitude, it seems God eventually gives me a revelation.

I'm well educated. I have two college degrees, and I've had a diverse career as an artist, producer, director, and manager in the corporate world. But at the same time, I'm no scholar or intellect. If it weren't for art classes, I would have never made it through college. I barely passed the required history, math, and English courses. I'm a scientific, "show me" and "prove it to me" kind of guy. I'm not the kind of person that can mix facts with imagination. Some of the testimonies I have are so far-out that I would not believe them myself if God had not given me witnesses and documentation.

Now at fifty-seven years old, I've been all over the world and done things I could never have imagined. I have seen and done so much in my life. But what good is it? Was it all just for me? Sure, I'm a different person than I would have been if all this hadn't happened to me. But, so what? What difference does that make in the whole grand scheme of things? I'm going to live and die just like everybody else, and when I'm gone, what did it really matter?

Ah, so here comes the revelation: I'm here to be a witness, to tell others my testimonies to demonstrate that God is real.

A testimony has to be absolute truth. You can't exaggerate it and make it sound better than it was, and you can't water it down to make it more believable. My testimonies in this book are the truth, and they are written with as much detail and accuracy as humanly possible.

Chapter 2

X MEANS "YES"

As a kid growing up in the 1950s, I thought I had a normal life, but then again, as a kid I didn't have anything to compare my childhood to. Now, looking back, I think there was one big difference in my life from the lives of other kids. From the time I was three until I was nine years old, my parents owned a small convenience store called Davidson's Confectionery.

In those days there were no grocery stores open on Sundays. Stores like 7-Eleven, Casey's, Quick-Trip, Mobil-Mart, or any other kind of gas-and-food shops, didn't exist yet. Our convenience store was open sixteen hours a day, seven days a week, selling the basic staple foods: canned goods, milk, bread, eggs, and fresh-sliced lunch meats. Today in our 24/7 society, that sounds very common, but back then it was rare. The state of Missouri had blue laws that restricted most businesses from being open on Sundays, so for us, Sundays were a gold mine.

Our store was a separate, small building next door to our little four-room house. We were located at a busy intersection in St. Louis County. Mom and Dad both worked in the store, plus my dad had a full-time job as a beer bottler for Anheuser-Busch. Even though my parents could make the short walk between our house and the store frequently, they relied a lot on my only sister, Velma, to help take care of me. Still, as early as pre-school age I can remember waking up alone in the house, getting dressed by myself, and walking over to the store say good morning to my mom.

Mom oozed love all over me. She always treated me like the most special kid on Earth. In fact, everyone was good and loving to me, even though I sure was a miserable, tantrum-throwing brat. I don't know why, and I'm not looking for any emotional or psychological explanations. I was just spoiled and insecure. I learned that if I pitched a big fit, I would get attention and get what I wanted. I can remember throwing myself on the floor kicking and screaming when I didn't even know what I wanted. And strangely enough, I can remember feeling bad and sorry while I was making such a scene.

With my parents working all the time, we had an unusual family life. We ate meals in a small room in the back of the store, with my parents taking turns waiting on customers while we ate. When I say it was a small room, I mean really small. It was only about six feet wide by eight feet long, with a sink, stove, table, and four chairs pressed against the walls on all sides. It was way more than cozy when the four of us were home to eat together.

I would have lots of time alone in the house. Frequently my parents would drop me off to spend a night or two in the city with my grandparents or my Aunt Dorothy. I stayed with my aunt so often she lovingly called me her adopted son.

We never attended a church, so my mom and dad never taught me about God, religion, or spiritual matters. My grandpa, who we called *Pop*, is the person responsible for my belief in God.

Pop and I spent hours and hours just riding around the old streets of St. Louis in his Nash Rambler. He told me story after story of the good old days when he was young. The stories included the good things as well as the bad—stealing, drinking, and where every red light district was—but he always managed to drop in a mention of God. It was Pop who taught me that God was real and that God would take care of me.

I can't remember Pop telling me any specifics about God. In fact, I'm certain there weren't any specifics. All Pop ever said to me was, "God is real," and "God will take care of you." That was all. But he repeated those two phrases enough to convince me they must be true.

No one in my family knew it, but as early as six or seven years old, I used to spend time alone in the partially finished attic of our house, just talking to this God who was taking care of me.

The nearest kids to play with lived on Arthur Lane, just a little way up the busy main road. They seldom came to play at our house due to the business at our store. Most of the time I had to go to their homes, and that made me feel like an outsider. They would tease me a lot and never let me feel like I was part of the gang. I'm not talking about all the kids. The girls were really nice to me. It only took the snubbing from two guys to make me feel different and left out.

Even at that young of an age, I was worried about what other people thought of me, and I wanted to fit in, not be different. That may have contributed to me relying so much on God at such an early age. God always listened, and He never teased me. It was really comforting to be with Him in that attic.

Without a church or Sunday school class to teach me, I didn't know who God was or how to pray, so I figured out my own way. I got the impression from Pop that we couldn't see God. I figured God would send us signs to let us know right from wrong, good from bad. I used to ask God simple yes-or-no questions that He could answer with a sign. I would take a small piece of paper and mark an X on one side of it. Then I would ask God a question and throw the piece of paper up in the air. If the paper landed on the floor with the X facing up, the answer was yes.

I wasn't always happy with the answers I got, but for a while this seemed to be working. It worked until I got stuck on one question: can I have a new bicycle? The answer was yes as often as it was no, but since the bicycle never showed up, I lost confidence in this practice and stopped doing it. Even though I no longer thought God was answering my questions, I still believed God was real and God would take care of me.

Chapter 3
NOT THIRTY, BUT FORTY FEET

On Christmas Eve in 1960 at just ten years old, a strange and long-lasting illness entered my life. I began having pains in my stomach around noon that day. It just felt like a bellyache at first, but throughout the day the pains increased. About eleven o'clock that night Mom called our family doctor, Dr. Hackmeyer, for help. Until that night he would have gotten in his car and come to our house. But instead, he informed Mom that he had joined the ranks of the other doctors at that time in history who stopped making "house calls." If we needed to see him, we were now going to have to wait and go to his office.

I was in such pain that Dr. Hackmeyer prescribed some medicine for me over the phone. Mom and Dad loaded me into the back seat of our car and we drove to downtown St. Louis to find the only pharmacy that was open all night for emergencies. I don't know if the medicine helped or if I just waited it out, but somewhere around four o'clock in the morning the pain stopped and I was able to get some rest.

That was the beginning of a condition we called "stomach attacks." I had a stomach attack once or twice every year since that Christmas but no one could ever determine the cause of the pain. The attacks were always the same: I would have such severe pains I would get bent over, crippled up, and rolled in a ball on a bed or on the floor for about sixteen hours at a time.

In the early 1960s I wasn't giving God much attention. No one in the family was talking about God or going to church. Occasionally my dad would listen to a preacher named Billy Graham on the radio. It sounded boring to me, so I never stayed in the room while it was on.

What I did hear sounded to me like preachers were part of a religion, a religion was believing in God, and God was three people in one. I wondered if that meant the God Pop said was real was really three Gods. Wow, was that confusing! I didn't get it—at all.

A lot of dramatic changes happened in my life in a short period of time. I graduated from a small grade school to a large junior high; my parents sold our store, so mom was home with me all the time; we moved from the tiny house to a bigger, ranch-style house; we went from the busy street in a commercial area to a quiet road with subdivision homes all around us; and my sister got married and moved out. I wish I could say my bratty attitude had gotten somewhat better by this time, but it hadn't. I was still acting mean and nasty to everyone in the family.

Mom and Dad's store had done well enough that we had a nice, big house; a white Cadillac in the garage; that new bike I had been wanting; a riding lawnmower; a TV that had a wireless remote control; an automatic garage door opener; and a small transistor radio with an earplug. Several of those items were new inventions for that day and time. With such new luxuries, I thought it made me a "somebody" in our new suburb.

With all that we had, it was easy to make friends in the new neighborhood. The friends I made were impressed with me (or rather, with all our stuff), so I thought it was my turn to get some of my peers back for treating me badly when we owned the store. My feelings were so hurt and injured that I wanted to get even. Suddenly I was the one teasing and putting others down. The only thing was, I was too young and stupid to realize I was taking it out on the wrong kids.

I'm ashamed to admit it, but even with all this prosperity, I used to steal one-dollar bills out of one of my friend's coin bank in his bedroom. I called him my friend, but actually I didn't like the guy. He was a nice, good kid, and I thought that was wimpy behavior for a guy. I didn't need any money. I think I stole from him for the same reason I used to throw tantrums and be so ornery to my family; I just didn't know what that reason was.

One summer day in 1962, some friends and I were playing in the woods around the subdivision and decided to build a tree house. The trees were tall, but none of them were big enough to build a platform in. Instead, we just nailed steps on one of the trees so everyone (even the girls) would be able to climb up.

I got several small two-by-four wood pieces nailed to the side of a tree when I realized they weren't going to work. There was no way to keep the steps from twisting and turning when you put weight on them, so I climbed up past the steps to see how high I could get, just on the branches alone. I looked down and Bob, Dan, Suzie, and Diane were all looking up at me. It was a little scary to be that high up, but I was the big man on the block now and intended to show everyone just how high I could get.

To get any higher, I was going to have to swing around to the other side of the tree. With both hands I grabbed a branch about one inch in diameter really tight and close, like I was holding a baseball bat. When I lifted my feet off the branch I was standing on, the branch I was holding tore clean off the tree and I fell backwards with it still clasped in my hands.

Falling at great speed, I could feel the other branches hitting my body as the ground was rushing up toward me, then all of a sudden it felt like my fall turned into slow motion. I saw a blast of bright light, and then I began to see pictures of myself. It was like watching a slide show. I saw myself from infancy all the way up to the present, one shot at a time. I saw my whole life. It seemed to be impossible to be suspended in the air that long.

Then I felt a hollow, empty feeling inside, like something was being sucked out of me, and by pure instinct I made a desperate plea to God. I didn't yell or speak out loud, but in my mind I said these exact words: "God, if you can save me from this, I promise to be good from now on."

When I hit the ground, I hit with such force that my body actually bounced! I almost landed on Diane. My head was turned sideways, and I was looking directly at her feet. I could see the surprised look on her face as I bounced up to about her chest, and then I was looking directly at her feet again as I landed the second time.

I didn't feel any pain, but I couldn't catch my breath. I had landed on my back, bent across a log that was about eight inches high. The fall knocked all the wind out of me. I jerked around for a few seconds, gasping for air. The fear of suffocating was terrifying. It seemed like forever, but I finally caught my breath and stood up. I still wasn't feeling any pain, but I couldn't find my left arm. I turned my head as far as possible, but my left arm was nowhere in sight. I twisted my body a little, and my arm unfolded like an accordion from up under my armpit and fell limp to my side.

At the sight of my arm, the girls took off running and screaming for help. The rest of us walked through several backyards in the subdivision to Bob's house. They sat me down in a lawn chair on his driveway and his mom called for an ambulance. When the ambulance and police arrived, they asked me how far I thought I fell. I told them it was probably about thirty feet, and they all laughed. The policeman said in a taunting manner, "Son, if you had fallen thirty feet you'd be dead."

The police had to measure the fall for an official accident report. From where the branch broke, it turned out to be forty feet to the ground. That's equal to a four-story building. Just inches away from where my head landed was a basketball-size rock.

I still wasn't feeling any pain and even waved good-bye to everyone as they strapped me down on a stretcher and put me in the ambulance. But, oh my, did that pain situation change. I ended up in a hospital bed for many hours without any medication or painkillers while the doctors ran tests to find all the injuries I had. I believe God let me have those hours of tossing back and fourth in excruciating pain to get my full attention.

My left arm was broken in three places, I had minor cuts and bruises, and landing with my back stretched over that log tore all the tissue away from the inside of my ribcage. The doctors said they couldn't set my arm without operating and inserting pins, so they needed to contact my dad at work.

Communication took a lot longer back then, than it does today. There was no such thing as a cell phone, so they couldn't just call my dad. Instead, they had to contact his employer, who had to physically send a messenger into the plant to find him. We had to wait hours for Dad to arrive in person at the hospital and give them permission to operate on me.

I was in the worst pain imaginable. It was unremitting and seemed to be in every inch of my body. As we waited for Dad, the only thing the doctors and nurses were doing for me was putting ice on my arm. I kept bellowing out pleas for help, for *somebody* to do *something* to get me out of the pain. Staring at the clock as the hours drug on and on was more than I could bear. Mom was right there at my side the whole time, but that was of little comfort. All she could say was, "You'll be alright," as she patted my head.

Once Dad arrived, they told him that without an operation I wouldn't have full use of my arm anymore. I can remember seeing Dad nod, but I didn't hear him say anything. He was always slow to respond. He always thought hard and long before he answered anyone about anything.

Finally, they put me to sleep to prepare me for surgery. When I woke up, there was a cast on my arm, but no operation. Mom said Dad's reply to the doctors (in his Tennessee slang) was, "Aw, I reckon we'll take our chances."

As for the rib tissue, I couldn't move my body at all without feeling like somebody was sticking a knife in my chest. Once I got home, it took six weeks of constant sitting up to heal. I wasn't even allowed to lie down to sleep. Dad put a piece of plywood under my mattress and elevated half of my bed to resemble a chair.

The cast on my arm was set up like a form of traction, so it had to hang free at the elbow at all times without resting it on the bed. In those six weeks I had plenty of time to remember the deal I made with God to be good and to remember Pop's words: "God is real," and "God will take care of you." In time, my arm healed without a problem. I have a slight loss of rotation in my left wrist today, but other than that, my left arm has been fine. Dad did well.

That accident started a change in me. I was determined to keep my commitment and be a good person, because I didn't ever want to have to go through an ordeal like that again. From that accident on, I stopped throwing tantrums and acting so mean. God did a work in me through that incident, because before it I didn't want to change. I didn't even know what to change or why I acted so badly. Afterward, I found that the older I got, the more sensitive I became for people other than myself, though that sensitivity was not enough to throw me into a real relationship with God. It was going to take something more serious than that—maybe another accident.

Chapter 4

SILENCE, LIKE IN A VACUUM

It was easy to think the slide show I saw while falling was just in my mind. We hear reports all the time about how much memory and ability our minds have that we don't ever tap into, so I gave my mind credit for that for a while. But the more time that passed, the more unnatural that slide show seemed to be.

While I was still recovering from that fall, my family was eating dinner one night and watching the evening news on TV. Most of it was about the war in Vietnam, until they got to the local topics. They reported that a man working in his garage fell off his six-foot step ladder and died. Died? He didn't survive a fall from only a few feet, and I fell four stories?

I knew something was going on. After all, your mind can't save your life. I decided that God must have really heard me and saved me during that fall, which meant God must be real. Pop was right!

If that were true, though, then what were my high school teachers talking about? I'd seen the skulls and other pictures in my science books. I could believe in evolution from ape to man, but they couldn't convince me it happened on its own or started by pure chance. I just figured God did the evolution. I accepted every science theory they threw at me, just by thinking God did it, but it was still a little confusing.

Early in the spring of 1969 something happened to me that I couldn't reason away with my mind. I was a freshman at Meramec Junior College. I had a terrible breakup with a girlfriend, Toni, just weeks earlier, and I was on my first date with Linda, a nice gal from one of my art classes.

I felt good. Linda had been expressing her interest in me while I was still dating Toni, and every guy needs that kind of boost for his ego, especially right after an ugly breakup. Linda introduced me to her circle of friends, and they invited us to a picnic at Babler State Park, not too far from campus.

I can't remember what month or what day it was, but I do remember it was cloudy, drizzling rain, and cold. We gathered at one of the rustic wooden pavilions in the park that was made of huge raw timbers and natural stones. It was just a roof over our heads with no walls, a big stone barbeque/fireplace at one side, and a couple of wood picnic tables in the middle. We mostly just hung out all afternoon, talking, joking, and acting up to entertain each other like a bunch of eighteen-to-twenty-one-year-olds would do.

Of course, someone of legal age brought some beer. I was only eighteen and wanted to be cool, so I was eager to have the chance to get a buzz. I didn't drink very much because I hadn't developed a taste for beer yet. It tasted awful, like soap water, to me. When no one was looking, I'd pour some out of the can to get done with it sooner and to fake everybody out so they would think I was drinking way more than I was.

From time to time, the wind would kick up and blow the cold, drizzling rain all over us. To keep warm, I pulled Pop's old wool army blanket out of the trunk of my car. We'd wrap it around us while standing or sitting, and when a gust of wind blew through, I'd throw it up over our heads and act silly for a laugh.

I wasn't very good at breaking the ice on first dates, so I put on more clownish behavior as I got more relaxed from the beer. Honestly, throwing the blanket over our heads was just my opportunity to sneak a kiss from Linda. At that age, I was too shy to kiss her in public like the cool couples were doing.

Around four in the afternoon, the party was breaking up and Linda and I got in my hot-looking '68 maroon Ford Mustang and headed for home. The roads in the park were nice, blacktopped roads with no traffic. However, the state roads that led to the park were narrow, concrete two-lane roads with no shoulders on the sides. This was back in the days before we had divided interstate highways in the area.

When I got to the state road at the exit of the park, I had good tunes blasting on the AM radio as I looked both ways for traffic before I pulled out. Linda was talking and laughing, and we were having a ball. I looked left and no cars were coming. I looked right and there was nothing in sight, but we were pulling out in the middle of a big curve in the road. To the right the road quickly disappeared as it curved behind the trees in the park.

Feeling cool and carefree, I casually pulled out onto the state road, making too wide of a turn, and crossed over the center line into the oncoming lane. Instantly, there was a huge tractor-trailer truck ahead traveling over the fifty mile per hour speed limit and barreling around the curve right at us. The truck was going so fast around the curve he couldn't stay in his lane. He was over the center line, too, coming straight at me, not even a car length away. It happened so fast I didn't have time to brake, jerk the steering wheel, or do anything. It was impossible to avoid the accident.

A great force of wind rocked my car violently from side to side. All my windows were rolled up, but we could even feel the wind hitting us inside the car. Like a flash of bright light, the truck zoomed right through us! Yes, I said *through us*. Not past us, but through us. I could actually see the truck in a faint, white, faded image, going right through the driver's side of my car. It was so loud, but the instant it was over, there was a dead silence. I hadn't turned the radio off, but there was an eerie, unnatural complete silence in the car—silence like in a vacuum.

Stunned, I looked in the rearview mirror to see the truck going so fast it was barely in sight. For a minute, we just coasted down the road looking straight ahead. I looked over at Linda and she was frozen still. We stared at each other, but didn't say a word. I can't remember us talking during the rest of the drive home.

I don't know if Linda experienced the same thing that I did or if she just thought we had a close call. I never came right out and asked her because this was our first date and I didn't want her to think I was crazy. On future dates with Linda, she never mentioned this event, so I didn't bring it up. For an eighteen-year-old, this was way too spooky to talk about to anyone, so I just kept it to myself. "After all," I thought, "who would believe such a thing?" I couldn't believe it myself, and I didn't want people to think I must have been drunk and imagined it. Or worse, I didn't want people to think I was nuts. You're not cool if you're a nut, and I wanted to be considered cool.

Just like during my slow motion fall from the tree, I had experienced a feeling like God had protected me, but this time I knew for a fact that some kind of unexplainable, supernatural thing had happened. I was certain this was not just a trick of my mind.

I know what you're thinking: maybe it was just a close call. But I was there, and I know there was no possible way that truck could have missed us. At that age, I had only been in church for weddings, never read a Bible story, and hadn't heard any formal teachings about God, other than the nativity story at Christmas. I didn't know God had supernatural powers presently at work, and I certainly didn't know He would use them on a guy like me. What I did know was that I had this indescribable "knowing" feeling, not just in my mind but in my whole being, that God was real, no matter what anyone else said.

I didn't want to believe the reality of what happened myself, until years later when I heard similar stories from other people. As you're reading, you can continue to try to explain these events away, or you can acknowledge them as facts that demonstrate how God supernaturally works in the world today.

Chapter 5
BOMBARDED

Growing up wasn't easy for me. I didn't have the ability to be my own person. I kept trying to fit in and be cool, like everybody else. Or at least be like the gang of friends I was hanging around with at the time.

Everybody likes to be liked, especially me, and trying to ride the fence and be bad with the bad guys and good with the good guys didn't work. My conscience would eat me alive when I hung around with guys who used to beat each other up and steal things for no reason, yet I felt like a sissy if I went to school functions and hung around with good kids and the scholars, or as we called them, the nerds.

As I was trying to get my own act together and figure out what life was all about, I often drove to Park Lawn Cemetery to have some heart-to-heart talks with Pop, who had died when I was seventeen. I figured that since Pop knew God was real, being at his gravesite might help me in some way to have a better connection to God. For about three years I frequently stopped by the gravesite around midnight to sit and talk. I might have been talking to Pop, but it was really just my way of praying to God.

After dating Linda at Meramec, I started seeing a blond cheerleader named Amy. Now, this was the first time I thought I found real love. Amy treated me like a god. No previous girlfriend had ever given me so much attention and made me feel so special. By the time I completed my associates degree, she and I had been dating steadily for a year.

To finish my college education, I had to move away from home to the University of Kansas in Lawrence, Kansas. Amy stayed in St. Louis, and for two more years we continued our relationship. We were tossing around the idea of engagement, but trying to hang on to each other while living apart and commuting five hours back and forth to keep dating was impossible. The physical distance between us took its toll, and we broke up before I graduated.

I was devastated. That was the most serious relationship I had ever been in with a girl. She had convinced me that I was everything to her, and then, boom, it was over. She didn't dump me for some other guy; she dumped me for *several* other guys. Well, that was great for her, but what was I supposed to do?

On the heels of that breakup with Amy, a series of coincidences started happening to me. On campus one day, a student who was a perfect stranger to me walked up and asked me if I'd like to come to a Bible study. I politely declined, but I thought he was a little goofy to do something like that.

A couple days later, another guy walked up to me while I was sitting on a bench outside of Strong Hall and asked me if I was saved. I tried not to talk to that guy at all, because I wasn't even sure what *saved* meant.

Meanwhile, I was feeling terribly lost and lonely over my breakup with Amy. I felt like my whole life was a mess. For the first time, I was so distraught over a girl that I cried, but I never would let anyone know it. As the days went by, I got more depressed. It wasn't so much the loss of Amy as it was the fear of building a new relationship with another girl that might also end some day. I didn't want to risk another heartache or rejection.

When I was feeling my lowest, another complete stranger walked up out of the clear blue and asked, "How ya doin'? Anything I can pray for you for?" I acted calm and said no, I was fine. But I was about to jump out of my skin! The chance of this happening to me almost every day on campus was getting to be too much to be coincidental. Was God trying to tell me something?

Before long I was on campus again and yet another unknown guy approached me. This guy was different. He was cool. He introduced himself as if he knew me from somewhere, so when he invited me to go to lunch with him, I was kind of curious to find out who he was. I thought maybe I had met him somewhere before.

He explained to me that he was operating his own business while he was attending school, and he'd like to tell me about it in case I might be interested in helping him. He had an official, legitimate-looking business card with some kind of logo on it. He was a likable guy, so I was willing to talk with him.

We made arrangements to meet at the Perkins Pancake

House just a few blocks away. It was early in the afternoon. I don't remember eating; I think we just had drinks. He began by telling me that he operated his business out of his apartment at night and there were several other guys who came there, too. He was kind of beating around the bush, so I started getting a little suspicious of his intentions. The longer he drug on, the more my caution flag went up. I began to suspect he might be some kind of a pervert with all his talk of the apartment, nighttime, and other guys.

He went on to explain that he taught classes, and he considered that to be his business, even though he didn't get paid to do it. At that, I had heard enough and started excusing myself. I kept telling him I had to get going, but he just kept talking and followed me out to my car.

As I opened my car door and started to get in, I heard him say that the classes he taught were about the Bible. I stopped dead in my tracks and turned to look at him. He was standing on the other side of my car, and I looked straight over the roof and stared him square in the eyes. At that moment, I felt an odd, warm, "oozy" feeling flow over me, and for some reason, I could tell that this guy was okay. He was sincere, and I could tell he knew God was real, too.

I kept his business card for a while, because down deep I wanted to step out and go to one of his classes to check it out, but I didn't have the courage to try something that new and unknown to me. It's a shame I can't remember his name. He made such an impact on me that I would love to be able to find him today and tell him so.

Not long after that luncheon, I was feeling so down I was literally sick to my stomach. There was a burning, gnawing feeling inside that almost felt like I had to throw up. I finally wanted to tell someone what was going on in my life and quit putting on a front like I was fine. The only friend who I thought would have any sympathy for me was my old buddy, Ron.

Ron wasn't exactly a good guy, but he was a good friend. I followed in his footsteps with a little shoplifting and vandalism when we were in our early teens. I'm not blaming him for being a bad influence on me, because again, it was me who was trying to fit in and be like him.

Ron was a most unique person. What I saw in him was his ability to be free and not worry in the slightest about being like anybody else. This was at the time in our American culture when the hippie era was starting to fade out, but Ron still fit the mold perfectly. He wholeheartedly adapted to living a lifestyle of peace, nonmaterialism, free will, free love, rock and roll, and drugs.

Ron experimented with all kinds of drugs, so his philosophies and views were "out there" to say the least—way out there. I am still amazed when I think about Ron's conclusion that since God is good, marijuana had to be good for you, too, since God created it.

Nonetheless, I knew if I could talk to anyone about my troubles without any inhibitions, Ron would be the one to talk to. But there was one big problem. Ron was such a free wheel he was constantly moving around between Missouri, Illinois, and Kansas, living in basements, abandoned farmhouses, trailers, or campers. He had moved so many times

I had no idea where he was. There was just no way I could contact him. I hadn't seen or heard from him in more than two years.

Miserable and crying, I knelt down in my bedroom and, looking out the window at the sky, I formally prayed, "God, if only I could talk to Ron, I could get over this awful situation and feel better." I barely got the last word of that sentence out of my mouth when the telephone started ringing. Before I answered it, I cleared my throat so no one could tell I had been crying. When I picked up the phone and said hello, I heard a familiar, sarcastic voice on the other end say, "Hey, man. What's up?" It was Ron.

If this had happened hours or days later, I would have believed it was just a coincidence, but there's no such thing as coincidence when it happens at the second you ask for it. I was shocked. God actually answered my prayer on the spot!

After spilling my guts to Ron about Amy, his only response to me was, "Man, I know. Well, how 'bout that?" With the condition I was in, even those words were comforting. When I got off the phone with him I had nothing else to do, so I walked into the living room and turned on the TV. It was almost evening on a Sunday in March or April of 1972. I had an old, portable black-and-white TV with only four or five channels on it. I flipped through each station, and on all the channels were preachers and church services.

I wasn't interested in listening to any of those kind of corny shows, but when I stopped searching, the last station had evangelist Oral Roberts preaching. Before I could turn the TV off, something struck me like a freight train. All

Oral Roberts said was, "God loves you," but it felt like he was talking directly to me. Everything he said after that seemed to be exactly how I was feeling and thinking at that very moment. It was uncanny. For the first time I realized those preachers do what they do because God is real to them, and they want everyone to know it.

At that moment I had an overwhelming notion that I should get to a church right away. I didn't know why, but it was urgent that I get to a church as soon as I could. I jumped up and scrambled around looking for a phone book. I looked up churches in the yellow pages and tried to pick one to go to, but I couldn't decide. I didn't know what the church names meant or what the difference was in the denominations, so I just got in my car and started driving around town looking for the right one. I drove past several and looked them over really well, but it just didn't feel right to park the car and go in.

When I turned the corner on to Massachusetts Street, there was a small building on the right that looked inviting. By this time it was dark out, so I could see people through the glass doors in front. I knew there must be a service going on inside. A red, neon sign out by the road read "Church of the Nazarene." I had no idea what that meant, but something was enticing me to go in.

As I parked my car and headed for the door, I realized I didn't have a clue what I was doing there. I couldn't anticipate what I was going to hear or see. My mind was thoughtless. It didn't even matter to me why I was there; I just had this unusual, instinctive feeling that I was supposed to be there.

It was quiet when I walked in. There were about fifteen to twenty men, women, and children scattered around in the pews. I don't remember any old people. Everyone seemed to be fairly young. The only sound I could hear was the pastor crying.

I sat way in the back where no one would notice or talk to me. It was a little uncomfortable being there, so I didn't think I would stay very long. I kept waiting for a sermon, but none came. Everyone but the pastor sat still and quiet. The pastor began to cry harder and started wailing. He paced back and forth across the pulpit with his Bible open in his hands as if he were reading it. Then others in the pews started sobbing. Some of them got out of their seats and laid down on the floor. Soon they began wailing, too, and rocking from side to side. I was stunned. What in the world had I gotten myself into?

Of all the churches in town, I picked the one that was full of nutcases! I had never seen such a sight before. I was ready to slip out the door when the pastor stopped pacing and began banging his head against the wall. Startled, I thought, "Oh my gosh! This man is crazy. I'm getting out of here."

By that time everyone was crying out and uttering hard-to-understand sounds—not words, but sounds—at the top of their lungs. I got up and started to run out, but guess what? I ran straight up to that pulpit and threw myself down at the pastor's feet. I began uncontrollable weeping and wailing myself, and to my surprise, I felt that warm, oozy feeling coming over me again.

The pulpit was a raised platform about two feet high. I knelt with my knees on the floor and my chest flat-out in the pastor's path. I have no idea how long I laid there. I remember trying to pray, but the only thing I could say was, "Thank you, God. Thank you, God." I kept trying to pray something, anything, but my mind was blank. All I could do was cry and keep repeating, "Thank you, God." I can't remember if the pastor touched me, prayed, or even spoke to me. I was so overwhelmed with such a good feeling of release that I never even looked up at him. When I stood up and turned around, I could see that a few people were gone and the overall volume level was a little quieter. The pastor was pacing again, and no one was paying any attention to me. I felt so relieved; it was like a thousand pounds had been lifted off my back.

Slowly I began to walk down the aisle, wiping the tears off my face and heading for my car. I felt so good; I wasn't in any hurry to leave. I got to my car, and before I started the engine, I burst out talking to myself about what had just happened. There I was, sitting in my car, laughing and talking out loud to God. I knew that my troubles were over and that God had much better things in store for me than I could ever imagine. God had given me the revelation that if my relationship with Amy had continued, I would have had a lot of heartaches and a miserable life, ending in divorce. I realized that breakup had to happen because God had something better planned for me. That is what Pop meant when he told me that God would take care of me.

This was no subtle little understanding I would have eventually come to on my own. It was different and had nothing to do with my mind or my thoughts. It was in my whole being, not in my head.

I left that church a changed person. That experience set me free from trying to fit in. I was less worried about what others thought of me, and it put a drive or need in me to tell others that God is real. I started my car and drove away with my windows rolled down, laughing and hollering at everyone I passed by. All the way back to my apartment, I was so excited I kept shouting out my car window things like, "Don't worry. God is real. God will take care of you."

Chapter 6

NAMES DON'T MATTER

DESPITE THE CHANGES THAT HAPPENED WITHIN me from that Nazarene experience, I still didn't feel like I needed to attend a church. I didn't even attempt to study or learn more about this God who was obviously helping and taking care of me. I was content with the fact that I knew He was real and that no matter what happened to me from then on, I knew everything would turn out okay.

Somewhere along the line, I decided on my own that I must be a Christian. I had no idea who God was or what was in the Bible; I just figured that since I believed in God and was a good person, that meant I was a Christian and would go to heaven. Then again, I was hearing a lot of reference to Jesus, and Jesus being the Son of God. It seemed Jesus was mentioned more often than God, and that didn't make sense to me. After all, if God really created a Son, wouldn't He, as the Creator, be more important than His Son, a part of His creation?

I heard the full name of Jesus Christ used a lot, too. I was so ignorant about the things of God that I thought *Jesus* was His first name and *Christ* was like referring to His last name. How embarrassing. I don't know when I finally realized that the term *Christian* was referring to the belief in Jesus *the* Christ. That was one of the reasons why I wasn't interested in going to a church. I didn't want to learn about being a Christian; I wanted to know more about being a "Godian."

Over time, I also got the impression that Catholicism was the largest and most important Christian denomination, and from that church I heard a phrase that really bothered me: "The Father, Son, and Holy Ghost." Holy Ghost? "Everybody knows ghosts aren't real," I thought. Why would people who believe in God refer to a ghost? And for them to say that God was really three gods in one made no sense at all. To me, God was God, not three gods.

I thought they must have gotten off on a tangent somewhere. I wondered how that church could have gotten so big, with so many members, if they were off base? Wouldn't God have shown them He is just one God, the Father of everything that exists? I was sure I was on the right track, all by myself. All I thought I had to do was just keep living my life doing what I thought was best, and let God keep doing what He does. Man, was I in need of some formal Christian education.

I graduated from KU in 1973 and moved back home with my parents. The economy was booming, jobs were plentiful, and in my vocation employers were outbidding each other to get me to come to work for them.

I took a great job as a technical illustrator for McDonnell Douglas Aircraft Corporation. I ran to the bank every Friday night and dumped my whole paycheck in my savings account at a time in history when even small, local banks were paying as much as 12 percent interest and giving you gifts like small appliances just for making a deposit. Life was good, with one exception: I was discouraged and tired of looking for a mate.

I hated the dating scene with a passion. I was not a competitive guy, and I had no intention to go out there and compete for a girl. At this point in my life, the only opportunities I had to meet girls were either at work or in a bar. I can remember being alone one night in a bar called John Henry's Railroad Cafe at Northwest Plaza Shopping Center. Sitting there sipping on a beer, I was mentally talking to God while watching all the other guys pouring themselves over every gal that walked in the door. And all the girls kept passing themselves around from guy to guy. Looking back, I can see that this was the main trouble I had with steady girlfriends. It was always just a matter of time until that next guy came along and the girl I thought was interested only in me would then show interest in someone else.

I had lost hope in finding someone who would be content to spend the rest of their life with the same person—me. I remember telling God: "I can't do this. I don't want to marry someone and maybe have that end someday, too.

So, God, if you have chosen me to be a bachelor, then that's okay with me. I'm done dating." I really thought I could get by without dating, but even though I told myself I was through searching for a potential wife, I kept asking God to send someone into my life who would never leave me or divorce me.

In no time, I was back in John Henry's Bar, but I really wasn't there looking for dates. I was there after work at night because the traffic on the highway was stop and go, bumper to bumper congestion for many miles. It took so long to drive home from work in that traffic that I could sit and socialize in the bar for hours and still get home close to the same time at night. The gang from work frequented this place daily, so we had our own meeting spot in a corner of the back room.

I noticed one of the same wild girls from work, Melainie, was there every time I dropped in. She was exactly the kind of girl I didn't like at all. She was way too outgoing and flirted with every guy in sight. One night, right before Thanksgiving, I must have mentioned that it was my birthday, which gave the whole gang a reason to celebrate. Somehow I left the bar that night having made a date to take Melainie to the show to see the hottest thing at the box office that weekend, *The Exorcist*. I scratched my head and wondered why in the world I made a date with someone so unappealing to me.

The Exorcist, with its rancid, demonic storyline, probably wasn't the best choice for a first date. It sure didn't help us ease into any kind of conversation. When I dropped her off at home that night, she mentioned to me that she was still dating a guy from the Air Force Academy. That was all I needed to hear to say good-bye to this gal. I proceeded to explain to Melainie that I wasn't looking for any kind of steady relationship. Actually, I was trying to drop the hint that I was not going to be asking her out again. She couldn't have cared less. She fired right back at me: "OK, but don't be so set that you miss the right one when she comes along."

That rattled me. I didn't like her at all, and yet she had the nerve to say something like that to me. It rattled me enough that I ended up asking her out again. We went on a couple more dates, but we weren't getting along very well. Every time she mentioned Tom, the Air Force guy, I was ready to take her home. He could have her. I wasn't interested in sharing a girl with another guy, and she didn't seem very interested in me anyway.

I was still asking God on a regular basis to send me a girl that would stick with me forever, and it was obvious to me that it sure wouldn't be Melainie. Just four weeks after our first date, I broke up with her during a Christmas party at my buddy Bob's house.

She didn't know anyone but me at the party. While I was running around having a good time, Melainie was left sitting alone with no one trying to make her feel welcome. When she finally had enough and wanted to leave, I decided I had enough of her. Even though we came to the party together in her car, I told her to leave by herself so I could stay there. I told her this was good-bye for good and that I didn't want to see her anymore, and she walked out the door.

To my surprise, she called me early the next morning. She said: "I can't believe you treated me like that. You might not want to date me anymore, but I'm not sure I'm done with you yet." I was dumbfounded. No girl had ever talked to me like that before. She reminded me that we had already made a date for a New Year's Eve party, and she wanted to know if I was going to honor that or not. Reluctant but curious, I agreed to keep that date.

New Year's was six days away, and we were both off work that week for Christmas break. All I can remember about those six days is getting together one night to play cards with my best friend, Steve, and his wife, Deb, at my parents' house. I invited Melainie to come that night, too, even though I knew Deb was trying to fix me up with her good friend, Jan. I didn't tell Melainie that Steve and Deb were going to bring Jan along with them that night.

The five of us played cards: Steve; Deb; me; and my two dates, Melainie and Jan. Deb and Jan weren't very nice to Melainie. In fact, they were downright mean to her. Still, Melainie treated them like they were her best friends. The nicer she treated them, the ruder they were to her. Melainie stayed until everyone else was gone that night and she never said one single word to me about Jan being there. She politely said goodnight, got in her car, and drove off.

After that night, I can't remember seeing or even talking to Melainie again before the New Years Eve's party. I picked her up and took her to a loud, crowded party in the basement of a small house. The host was one of the guys from work, and guess who showed up at the party? God. That warm, oozy feeling flowed all over me again, and I got that inner knowing. This time I just knew that Melainie was the girl I'd been praying for. I felt strange, not very coherent but most confident. While dancing a slow dance with her and without forewarning, I unemotionally and very nonchalantly asked her if she wanted to get married. I wasn't a bit surprised when she said yes.

Talk about a 180-degree turn! We had dated for four weeks, broke up for one week, and then got engaged. From that night on we were so infatuated with each other it was like a Hollywood movie. We smiled and laughed so hard at each other all day long that my jaws ached when I went to bed at night.

We both wanted to get married as soon as possible, but she was a member of the United Church of Christ. Their traditions wouldn't allow us to get married during the season of Lent. We were going to have to wait three months.

One Friday night I took Melainie to a party to meet some more of my friends, Sal and Roz. They were already married, and they were sure I was a confirmed bachelor. I had forewarned Sal and Roz that I was engaged, but they thought it was a joke.

Once we arrived at the party, I called for everyone's attention so I could officially make an announcement. It went like this: "Okay, everybody, I'm not kidding. I'm really going to get married. I'd like you to meet my fiancé, Melainie… Melainie…?" I didn't know her last name. I was engaged to her and didn't have a clue what her last name was.

Well, that really broke the house up. What a laugh they got out of that! They were certain it was just my hormones talking marriage. As for Melainie, she thought I was joking around, too. She thought I was kidding about not knowing her last name, but I didn't even know what initial her last name started with. If I was going to marry someone and not even know her name, then it had to be God.

One of the groomsmen for our wedding was far-out Ron, and he was really concerned for me. He showed up at my house the day of our wedding to warn me. He usually showed up drunk or stoned, but for this occasion he was exceptionally sober.

He began by expounding in his lofty manner: "You know, with the inert nature of human beings, it is incomprehensible for people to expect to stay emotionally or physically bonded to another person for their entire existence on earth." (Ron always liked to talk deeply like that.) Then he more brashly said, "You're gonna get married? You've only known this gal a few weeks. What are you gonna do if this doesn't work out?"

I chuckled a little bit and stopped getting dressed in order to look him right in the face and replied, "I have been praying for this. There's no way this won't work. When you hear from God, you just know it." Well, Ron let me know what a fool he thought I was to talk like that, because he had come to the conclusion that God was some kind of cosmic energy and not a force that gets involved with such trivial human matters as marriage.

So, was I hearing from God to do such an impulsive thing with someone I barely even knew? To date, Melainie and I have been married for thirty-four years, and it's been the best thing that's ever happened to me. I never could have imagined that marriage would be so much fun. Just when Melainie and I think our marriage can't get any better than it already is, it does! She's not only my best friend, but next to God, she is my reason for living.

Chapter 7
I GUESS SO

As a newlywed, there are always some surprises about the person you married. With Melainie, the surprises were always good ones. On the other hand, I unintentionally had a surprise for Melainie that was a bit shocking. After only a few months of marriage, Melainie woke up in the middle of the night to find me doubled up in a ball on the floor and groaning.

When she asked me, "What in the world is wrong with you?" I began to fill her in on my painful battle with the stomach attacks that had been afflicting me since I was ten years old. She then blurted out, "Are you kidding me? What are you talking about? Why didn't you tell me about this before now?" The only reply I could come up with was, "Uh…I don't know. I just didn't think about it."

Within a few minutes of that conversation, Melainie was driving me to Alexian Brothers Hospital Emergency Room. This wasn't the first time I had to be hospitalized for stomach attacks. I had been hospitalized several times and had every test know to medical science performed on me, but the doctors could never find the cause of the pain.

When I was young, they thought the pain might be some form of epilepsy. Over the years they changed the diagnosis to appendicitis and removed my appendix. After the appendix operation, the diagnosis became hypoglycemia, then gastritis, and then colonitis. Every time I was hospitalized and tested the diagnosis and treatments changed, but nothing ever relieved or cured the condition.

The stomach attacks were always as consistent as clockwork. They always happened once or twice a year. They always started with a faint pain in my upper stomach area around noon. The pain got increasingly worse all day long. By midnight I would be in such pain I would be doubled up and immobilized. By two o'clock in the morning I would be out of my mind with pain, unable to bear it any longer. It was usually at this point when Melainie would drive me to the hospital.

After reviewing the history in my medical records, the hospital staff would give me an injection of a pain medicine and send me home. By four o'clock in the morning I would be getting enough relief from the pain killer to get some sleep. The next day my stomach would be so sore it would hurt just to walk around, and it took two or three days for the soreness to go away. It was exactly the same scenario every time.

I Guess So

After a few years of marriage we were putting in long hours working in different careers at different places, so Melainie and I always had lots of notes to compare. Every night we would play catch-up with each other and briefly talk over some of the day's events. We'd do this lying in bed in the dark, right before we'd roll over and go to sleep. Usually, Melainie would fall asleep while we were talking, and I would lay there awake for hours contemplating everything we talked about.

In our late twenties we were partying heavily, going everywhere, and buying and doing everything that made us happy. After we got married, we were probably the first couple in our gang of friends to lose interest in drinking parties and the reckless behavior that came with it.

In the workplace, we noticed a lot of people had girlfriends or boyfriends at work, besides their spouses at home. Then you had wars, disasters, and less fortunate people suffering all over the world. These kinds of issues would come out in our catch-up at night, along with the petty stuff like who said what, to whom, or what one of us saw at the mall.

Before Melainie would doze off, I would tell her about the notions I would get in my mind and how the answer to any of the issues we discussed would always revolve around God. I can remember lying in bed after she had fallen asleep thinking to myself, "Where am I coming up with this stuff? Who the heck am I to say such things? I don't know anything about God, so how can I be telling others about Him?"

I felt like I could talk about God around Melainie because she went to Sunday school as a kid and grew up in a church family. I did this same thing with my coworkers, my subordinates, and my superiors without even knowing if they were church people or not. If they were having a problem, a need, or a tragedy in their lives, I would comfort them by telling them that God is real and God would take care of them. I would even tell them about God having supernatural powers to help them when it seems there is no hope. I didn't get these ideas from hearing them preached. It was just that to me, there was no other answer.

A couple years later Melainie was working as a service order writer for Southwestern Bell Telephone, and I was working as a technical artist for Communico Incorporated. At Communico, we met Keith and Julie, who became two more of our best friends. To get better acquainted with each other, we met up one night at Concord Bowling Alley for a little socializing. We barely knew either of them at this point, but we hit it off really well. After bowling a few games and having a lot of fun, we started getting ready to leave. We stood at the top of a staircase making plans to get together again when, for no apparent reason, Julie said to me, "You're a born-again Christian, aren't you?" I replied: "Uh, yeah. I guess so," and Julie said, "Oh, I could tell by the things you said."

Things I said? "What did I say?" I wondered. We were just bowling, for pity's sake. Nobody said anything about God that I could recall. I was alarmed with myself. I thought I must have shared some of my self-made theology during the night. I had no idea what I might have said earlier, and I didn't know what a born-again Christian was. I just thought it meant I believed in God, so I replied, "I guess so."

Those words, *born again*, had an immediate impact on me. When Julie said those two words I remembered

I Guess So

that awakening experience I had at KU. I might have been looking right into Julie's face when I said, "I guess so," but I wasn't seeing her face at all. I was seeing myself walking out of that little Church of the Nazarene, laughing and shouting that God is real. Is that what Julie meant? If Julie could tell I believed in God, did she know I had never read a Bible or gone to church?

Chapter 8
SICK AND TIRED

As a young adult it seemed like I had the world by the tail. I was driving around in a new Corvette sports car, had a metal-flake speedboat, was building a new house in a lake subdivision, and worked in an industry similar to advertising. Sounds exciting, right? It was so exciting and so much fun that I drove myself to a nervous breakdown.

In the spring of 1978 I was at a car dealership picking up a new Dodge van when I caught my salesman in a lie. The woman being helped in line before me was having her van undercoated, and the price they were charging her was much less than they charged me for the same thing.

When I confronted my salesman with the issue, I suggested that there must be some kind of mistake. He said, "No, that's the price it's supposed to be." When I asked why she was paying less, my salesman just shrugged his shoulders and said I would have to ask his manager. He escorted me to his manager's office and sat me down in a chair. Rather than admit what they did, they tried to avoid the real issue of price by saying I was accusing them of being liars. I never said or even insinuated any such thing. In fact, I remained silent the whole time as the manager argued with himself.

The manager got so upset with my silence that he finally screamed, "Throw this guy out of here!" At that, I got up out of the chair and walked over to a salesman's cubical on the showroom floor. I asked to use a phone and called Melainie to tell her what happened. I wanted her opinion on whether I should let them get away with this or ask to see the owner of the dealership.

While I was dialing the phone, my hands started shaking and my whole body started to tremble. By the time Melainie answered, I was sick to my stomach, and I could barely talk. She had no idea what was going on, and I had no idea what was wrong with me. I was dazed and confused. I couldn't think clearly or make sense of anything I was saying, so Melainie had to leave work and come pick me up.

Over the next few days I bounced back and forth from feeling normal to getting whacked-out and over-reacting to everything. The shaking became more of a constant trembling. It got so bad that I couldn't hold a pencil in my hand, and at the slightest sudden noise, like a doorbell or telephone ring, I would jump out of my skin and shake violently all over.

I ended up going to a doctor, who informed me that it was my nerves. I had driven myself too hard to be good, to be liked, to be successful, to be the best. They medicated me and set me up for counseling sessions. This went on for almost a year, and I wasn't getting much better. I kept working during this time, but it was difficult to function very well in my new position as a manager of a group of specialized artists. I lost hope in the doctors because the shaking only went away while I was on medicine. The counseling sessions went down like a grade school psychology class—very unprofessional. The only thing the counselors were concerned with was if I felt like killing myself, which I wasn't.

I eventually quit my job because the counselors suggested that my jittery nerves would calm down if I changed to a less stressful occupation. Boy, was that the wrong thing to do. I quit in the dead of winter and started hunting for a new career. Just imagine a nervous, spacey artist with trembling hands at a job interview to be a Xerox copier repairman. Any wonder no one wanted to hire me?

I spent three scary months with no job. Getting up alone each morning in a big, empty house, I was feeling like I lost it, like I was a reject—like I didn't have what it took to make it in the business world. That was the longest, most miserable three months of my life.

Out of sheer desperation to get well, I decided that if those doctors couldn't get me over my symptoms, then I would find someone who could. I remembered what going to that little Church of the Nazarene had done for me, so as a last resort, I decided I would try talking to a pastor. I picked up the phone book and called a church nearby that my mom and my aunt had gone to on holidays. I made an appointment with Pastor Bill Richardson at the Pacific United Methodist Church. We talked for a few minutes, and Pastor Bill grinned. Looking at me with a smirk on his face, he said, "Doctors and medicines can help you, but they can't heal you. Only God can do that."

It was like somebody hit me on the head! How could I forget what Pop taught me? How could I be telling others that God could take care of everything and not apply that to my own health? Pastor Bill didn't ask me to come to one of his services, read the Bible, or even pray. He just told me to throw the nerve medicine away and trust God. And that's what I did. I went straight home, threw the medicine in the trash, and never went back to a doctor or counselor for my nerves ever again. The shaking soon stopped, and I found I had more confidence and self-control than ever before.

From that meeting on, I had a desire to go to church and find out who God is and how He works. I took a temporary freelance job with Busch Creative Services, an Anheuser-Busch subsidiary. Soon I was asked to hire on full-time, and within three years I had been promoted several times, all the way up to an executive position as manager of administration. I wasn't seeking those promotions. I was trying to avoid them. The more I got promoted, the more stress came along with it, and I was anxious enough without more responsibility. However, the money was great and the job was fun, loads of fun.

I worked with movie stars, politicians, and some of the top entertainers of the day. I traveled all over the world, first class. With the sixty to eighty-hour workweeks necessary to produce multi-media shows, plus the stress of the corporate world wanting everything done yesterday, I developed another health problem.

This time it wasn't my nerves. At thirty-one years old I was diagnosed with multiple bleeding ulcers, possibly due to acid in my stomach from lack of sleep. The stomach attacks finally made sense. I was probably forming ulcers all along. I went to a series of doctors until I was finally referred to a specialist, who said that if the bleeding couldn't be controlled, they would have to operate.

To determine if operating was necessary, they performed another endoscopy, which meant inserting a tiny camera down into my stomach. I got to look at the endoscope picture myself while the camera was still inside me. The doctor said the round, pink background was my stomach and any white spots are ulcers. What I saw in that camera scared me. My stomach was mostly a white background, with just a small pink area. My condition was severe, too much so to operate. The advice from the doctors for recuperation was to avoid stress. They suggested that I change my lifestyle. This did not just mean not working too hard. It also meant I couldn't get too happy or too excited about anything. Good things or bad things—both are considered stressful on the body, and both dumped too much acid into my stomach.

At the time I was regularly attending a church and earnestly seeking God by listening to the sermons and trying to apply the messages to my life. I started to think God was speaking to me through my repeated health problems to give me a reason to escape the hectic corporate world and start serving Him in some way. I didn't know what "some way" meant, but I was willing to try and find out.

The only hang-up was how Melainie was going to react to this news. She had been listening to all my God-talk over the years and received it well, but to quit my job and go serve Him? I thought that was for pastors and special people called by God, not just some average, ill husband like me—and especially not someone who had never read a Bible.

Melainie was a rut person. Change didn't come easy for her, and she had always been very blunt with her opinions. She had a clear compassionate side, but it wasn't openly displayed. By this time we'd been married nine years, and from my experience with her, I was sure her reaction was going to be, "Are you nuts?" One night we were sitting on the couch facing each other in a quiet house. With no TV on and the dog on my lap, somehow I managed to slip into the conversation an announcement about quitting my job to serve God. I'm glad she didn't ask me what "serve God" meant, because I didn't have an answer for that. Melainie just stared straight ahead. The only sound out of her was, "Humph." She said nothing else about it.

Now, "humph" was a good sign; it left the door open. I did a quick study of our finances, and with her latest promotion as a project manager for Southwestern Bell, we agreed that we could get by on one income for a while. I resigned from my position at Busch and left the fast-lane behind.

In 1984 Reverend A. D. Van Hoose was a guest speaker at our church. He invited everyone in our congregation to join him on a mission trip to Haiti, where he operated an orphanage for boys. When this invitation was made, my first reaction was, "Not me; I'm sick. I'm not going anywhere."

Melainie brought the handout literature about the orphanage home with her. She slipped it to me and said,

"I think you should call them. I think you should go." It was very unlike her to want me to go. I had traveled a lot for Busch, and Melainie hated every minute of it. She never wanted to me to be away from home, not even for one night. On the other hand, I thought, "OK, I've got plenty of time on my hands. I'll be a good Samaritan and go help build a concrete-block school building in Haiti."

I signed on for the team and met up with the rest of the volunteers in Evansville, Indiana. There were a couple women and about nine or ten men, including myself. Some of the team members took a plane to Miami to catch our intercontinental flight to Haiti, but those of us on a lesser budget piled into a nine-passenger van and drove to the Miami airport.

Along for this mission were Reverend A. D. Van Hoose and his son, Reverend Rick Van Hoose. They pastor their own church in Evansville. Most of the team were either a part of the Van Hoose family or congregation members.

I had only been attending a church for three years myself, but in that time I had developed the opinion that pastors and men who called themselves Christians were more refined or dignified than the average person. I thought men of God had to be serious, reserved, and more sophisticated than the average man. So I thought being a volunteer missionary was going to put me in the presence of holy, somber men. Well, not these guys. They told jokes, argued at times, and acted like regular, everyday Joe's, like myself. That was a relief in one way, but I questioned myself as to how much they could know about God and still act so normal.

Haiti has the reputation of being one of the most poverty-stricken nations on Earth. Even though I had traveled overseas for business, this was my first time to experience a third-world country beyond the tourist spots. When we arrived in Haiti and stepped out of the plane, the first thing I noticed was the stench of urine in the air. It was so strong it about knocked me over. Walking down the sidewalks of the city streets we had to stay a couple feet away from the buildings. Raw sewage from drain pipes dumped right out of the sides of the buildings onto the sidewalks at just about shoe height. To avoid getting wet feet or legs, we couldn't walk too close to the buildings.

I had seen plenty of poverty on television, but walking in its midst was gut wrenching. Scarcely clad, ragged, dirty, hungry, handicapped people were everywhere. With their teary eyes and sad faces, it was no longer just a scene on TV, but a painful reality that made me sigh heavily.

Haiti only had two classes of people: rich and poverty-stricken. Throughout the countryside you see large mansions protected by stone walls around all four sides. Along every inch of those walls are cardboard, tin, and straw huts pressed together in an endless chain. Naturally there was crime in Haiti, but their motive for crime was purely survival, not greed. They stole food, not luxuries. The Haitian security had a very effective means of crime prevention there. If you got caught stealing a piece of fruit or loaf of bread, they cut off your hand.

At the worksite of the boy's orphanage there was no machinery; everything had to be done by hand. It was like going back a hundred years in time. The work was hard. My job was to dig foundation footings in the hard-packed clay soil with a hand pick and shovel, and transport concrete for the footings over the rough terrain in a wheelbarrow. This strenuous physical work was not the thing to be doing with a sensitive, bleeding stomach.

Well, sure enough, about halfway through this mission, I suffered from the most severe ulcer illness I ever had. The medicine I brought with me was doing nothing for the pain or bleeding. I couldn't work, walk, or even move. I told Randy, one of the other men on the team, about my illness and that I would have to stay in bed that day instead of helping at the building site. Randy lightheartedly said, "No problem. We'll just get the guys together and lay hands on you in prayer. That way, you'll get healed and never have this problem again."

Randy was serious, but his attitude seemed so frivolous, it turned me off. I politely thanked him and told him that I would rather not do that. Besides, these were plain old guys. How could they heal anybody?

I lay awake all that night. The relentless pain was in the upper part of my stomach near my rib cage. It wasn't a burning pain. It felt more like the pain from a smashed finger or toe. It got worse, to the point I knew I was in serious trouble. The doctors had informed me that if my ulcers continued to get worse, they could become life-threatening, so I began to have thoughts like, "If I die here, I'll never see Melainie again." That thought drove me to submission.

The next morning, I sheepishly asked Randy to go ahead and get the other guys together to pray for me. There I was lying on an old army cot in an old army building in a remote, foreign country with five strange men circling around me, praying. They started making strange sounds like the ones I heard in the Nazarene church. I learned from working with these men that they were speaking in "tongues," but that way of praying was most uncomfortable for me. To have them lay their hands on me was embarrassing. I wanted it to be over, and I wanted them away from me. I was sorry I caved in and asked them to do it.

The crowning insult came when one of the guys pulled out an empty bottle of Mazola Cooking Oil. I thought, "Oh, good grief. They're going to anoint me with cooking oil? What a joke!" I was looking up through the bottom of the bottle. I could see a finger lashing from side to side trying hard to get a slight trace of oil. I watched that finger as it came down and touched my forehead. I can remember talking to God in my head and thinking, "OK, God, I'm just going to listen to these guys and see if I think there really is anything to this."

At the instant that finger touched me, a cold sensation spread over my whole body. I was tingling all over and the room started to spin around in a circle. I felt a sensation like a cold rubber band around my forehead, and I could feel that rubber band moving slowly down my body until it seemed to lift, or disappear, out of my toes. As the band was moving down my body, I could feel the cold pain below the band and a warm, comfortable feeling above the band.

Then I felt like I was lifted up, way high up in a corner of the room. I could see the whole room from a bird's-eye view. I could see all the guys standing around me, and I could even see myself lying on the cot. All the men's prayers fused into one sound, and I started praying myself. I don't remember what I prayed, but everything went black when I did. It was as if I passed out. When I came to, I was alone. I don't know how long everyone stayed in the room or when they left me, but I could tell I had been out for most of the day because it was getting dark outside.

I got up when it was time to eat dinner and felt a strange sensation. It felt like my head was detached from my body, as if my head were a balloon floating and bobbing on a string a few feet behind me as I walked along. My first thought was, "Oh, man, those guys must have drugged me or something." Also, my stomach felt numb. The pain was so dull it was hardly noticeable.

When the first person walked up and spoke to me, I can remember replying to them in slow motion. I could hear myself talking extremely slow and in a deep, distorted tone, like when you play a record on slow speed. I asked people about this the next day, and they said I was talking and walking perfectly normal. Something else I noticed the next day was that I didn't have any pain in my stomach and the bleeding had completely stopped. I had been passing blood constantly and heavily for the past three years, but that day I wasn't bleeding. I didn't have any bleeding or pain the next day, or the next day, or any day after that.

God had miraculously healed me, and He used a bunch of common men to do it. God is real!

When I got home from Haiti, I was so excited that I told everyone about how I had received a healing and didn't have bleeding ulcers anymore. I was expecting everyone to be elated and get as excited as I was, but other than Melainie, most people's reaction was not what I expected. In fact, there wasn't much reaction at all. People just said things like, "Mmm, good for you," or "Oh, that's nice," and went about their business like they didn't hear a word I said. Most of them wouldn't even look me in the face. I thought everyone was going to be thrilled with my announcement, not put-off by it. Talk about a wake-up call.

Chapter 9
GHOST VS. SPIRIT

Even though I was attending a church every week, the only education I was getting was from the Sunday sermons and Scripture readings. You would think receiving a healing like I did would have at least prompted me to read a Bible, but nope, not me. I thought, considering what God had already done for me without officially studying, why would I need to start? On the other hand, Melainie was getting involved with the church in a big way. She was not just going to classes, but helping teach them as well. The growth in her understanding of spiritual matters was kind of intimidating for me, the man who thought he could learn without the help of others.

Melainie was going for it. She was on fire in her search for God. The more she studied and the more she read, the more adamant I was about not studying. She prayed and talked to God on her own, and I did the same; but though we both believed in God and attended church together, we never prayed together. For some reason, I could pray with others, but not with my own wife. That just wasn't comfortable for me. She could verbalize thoughts and prayers much better than me. I talked like a country bumpkin.

While Melainie was studying to learn more about God, I went off with another mission team to experience God firsthand in Israel. I went with the same pastor that took me to Haiti, Rev. Rick Van Hoose.

My function on the team was to be the camera operator. I recorded and edited audio and videos of Reverend Rick presenting mini-sermons on location so that he could use them for his televised services. We shot clips all around Jerusalem, Bethlehem, Jericho, and many of the notorious biblical places throughout Israel. One of the clips we needed to shoot was in the famous Upper Room. In the Bible, that is where the Day of Pentecost took place, when the sound of a mighty rushing wind was heard and tongues of fire came from heaven and rested on the heads of the apostles.

When we first arrived in the Upper Room, we gathered in a circle for prayer. An old gentleman from Reverend Rick's church was along with us. He was either in his late seventies or early eighties. When we opened our eyes after praying, the old man was leaning forward at about a thirty-degree angle to the ground with his eyes still closed. Very, very slowly he rocked forward and then backward, to such an extreme angle that it appeared to be against the laws of physics. He should have fallen down.

Somebody on the team reached out to catch the man, but Reverend Rick softly told us not to touch him because he was in the Spirit. The man swayed like that for quite a while, and then he stood up straight and opened his eyes.

He looked around the circle at all of us staring at him and asked, "What's going on?" He had no recollection of anything since we walked into the room. We told him what had just happened and that it wasn't possible to lean that far without falling. The old guy didn't say a word. He just raised his eyebrows and walked off like it was no big deal.

We were in the Upper Room to reshoot what had already been done on a previous trip there. When they got home with the first video it was blank, and all they had on the audio was a sound like rushing wind. I reshot Reverend Rick's six-minute sermon, and I made darn sure it recorded properly this time. I could see him in the monitor, and I watched the UV meters closely to adjust the sound level properly.

Reverend Rick and I would go over all the shots every night in our hotel room to see what they looked like. That night, when we reviewed the shot in the Upper Room, the video was blank—again! There was nothing to see, and on the audio there was nothing but a sound like a violent wind blowing through the room, just like on the Day of Pentecost. After a brief pause of silence, Reverend Rick looked down at the floor, shook his head, and mumbled, "OK God, I get the message. I guess I won't try recording that again."

While at the Jordan River in Tiberius, I had the opportunity to get baptized again. Even without proper study, I had learned from sitting in church on Sundays that to be a Christian I had to confess my belief in Jesus. I also knew I needed to be baptized. Melainie's church required me to get baptized before they would marry us, so I did. They had a nice, quick baptism ceremony for me. They sprinkled my head with water, and I repeated whatever they asked me to say. But it didn't mean a single thing to me. Nada. Zilch. Nothing! I was just doing it to get married. At that time I thought it was just a man-made tradition that had nothing to do with God, and I was very anti-traditional about everything.

While we were in Israel, we were at the place where they think John may have baptized Jesus. I was certain that if ever there were a special place where God would do something supernatural or holy, that would be it. After having that out-of-body experience getting healed in Haiti, I was expecting God to do something really wild and mind-blowing during this baptism.

The spot was an official tourist baptism location, complete with a handrail so you didn't fall while walking out into the river. We walked past a pastor who completely submerged us, one at a time. When I went down under the water, I was thinking, "Oh, boy, this is it." I was expecting to see a dove or at least a bright light or something, but I was most disappointed when nothing happened. What really bugged me was that I didn't even get that warm, oozy feeling that I was anticipating. Tradition or not, at least this time I knew what I was doing, and I meant it.

Near the end of our trip we traveled to a kibbutz, a communal farm in Hagoshrim on the border of Lebanon. It was eerie and very sad to see all the children in their schools practicing bomb drills like children in America practice fire drills.

For our sleeping accommodations, I got paired up with Reverend Rick again. In our room that evening, I began to share what my expectations were from my baptism in the Jordan. That lead me into a long speech on my understanding of God and why I think most people don't truly believe God is real. As I kept talking, that warm, oozy feeling started coming over me. I noticed Rick's mouth was hanging wide open. I didn't know if he was bored stiff or amazed by my crazy notions of God. As it turned out, he was amazed. He broke in and interrupted me with these three words: the Holy Spirit.

We both paused for a moment and then Rick continued, "I think you were quoting from the first and second chapters of Romans, about how there is no excuse for not believing in God because we see Him revealed to us in nature. Man made God into the image of creatures—cows, fouls, etc.— and worshiped the creature more than the creator. You were speaking under the anointing of the Holy Spirit and were surprising even yourself with profound statements that made good sense biblically without having a background for making such statements."

I was dumbfounded. Me? Roy Davidson? I was a nobody. I didn't understand why God would anoint a nobody like me with the Holy Spirit, but when Rick, an intelligent, ordained reverend told me this, I knew that I wasn't making stuff up. I wasn't crazy. I was hearing from God. All the notions and ideas I was getting about God over the years were true. "So this was what that inner knowing was," I thought. It was impartation.

It was that night that I came to understand how God speaks, or imparts, knowledge directly to people through His Holy Spirit. There is an unmistakable difference between the thoughts of your mind and the voice of God speaking to you in the Spirit. That night I understood for the first time the concept of God being three in One and the phrase "Father, Son, and Holy Ghost (Spirit)." I had to admit those Catholics I used to watch on TV knew what they were talking about, after all.

Reverend Rick rolled over and went to sleep. I just rolled over. In fact, I rolled and rolled all night long with the excitement of what had just happened. I couldn't wait to get home and tell Melainie, and I couldn't wait to start reading the Bible for the first time and find out more about what I had just quoted.

Chapter 10

BLACKOUT

I DUG INTO READING THE BIBLE FOR THE FIRST TIME in March of 1984. It took me nine strenuous months to read every page. That was the main reason I didn't want to read it in the first place.

Reading was so laborious for me that I picked up a set of Bible cassette tapes. Every night I would fall asleep with my headphones on, listening to one of those tapes. I also listened to teaching cassettes from Pat Robertson, whom I had grown to respect from his TV ministry, *The 700 Club*.

I even went so far as to go to a Bible study class with Melainie. Unfortunately, the class presented more questions for me than answers. I didn't understand how there could be so many versions and interpretations of the Bible if it was really God's Word. The class discussions revolved around commentaries that numerous authors had written books about. Many had a slightly different explanation of what a certain passage meant, and some of them even contradicted each other. I didn't want someone else's opinion of who God is. I wanted the correct version, from God Himself. Throw in all the different denominations of Christian churches and the debating over who's right and who's wrong, and I was overwhelmed. I was afraid all that information would cause me to doubt my belief in God instead of confirming it.

Melainie, on the other hand, read everything she could get her hands on and attended every meeting she could get to. She was leaping way ahead of me in her knowledge of Scriptures, biblical facts, and doctrines. Since we were in a Methodist Church, she was trying to learn Methodism while I was trying to learn "Christianity."

A couple weeks after returning home from Israel, I had to take a trip back to Reverend Rick's church to finish some editing of the videos we made. I traveled there and back by myself, so I had a few hours alone in the car each way to think while driving.

My thinking led to doubt. My mind was telling me, "Come on now, Roy, you think this rubber band story of a healing really happened to you? Are you sure you weren't letting your imagination get a little carried away? As smart as you are, do you think it was praying to God that healed you, or was it the medicine you had been taking?"

I was driving down I-64 in the daytime at seventy miles per hour as I battled those thoughts back and forth. I began to feel foolish for telling people that I had received a miraculous healing from God. I was looking straight ahead at the car right in front of me when my sight went totally black. I was blind as a bat. I couldn't see a thing. At the very moment everything went black, I felt that same rubber band feeling on my forehead that I had felt in Haiti. This time the rubber band moved slowly down my body to my stomach, where all the pain used to be. I could feel that same cold feeling below the band, and the same warm feeling above it. It was identical to the feeling I had during the healing, with one exception. This time, when it got to my stomach it stopped and reversed direction. It came back up my body to my forehead and lifted away.

The whole time this was happening I was scared to death, expecting to crash into something any minute. Since I couldn't see a thing, I was afraid to turn the wheel or hit the brakes. I had taken my foot off the gas and had a death grip on the steering wheel, hoping to keep the car straight in my lane. Much like the slow motion fall from the tree, it seemed impossible to be blinded for so long while zooming down the road.

Slowly, the blackness cleared up. When I could see again, there was no car in front of me anymore, and there was no car behind me. The only cars in sight were on the other side of the median, going in the opposite direction. I looked around, but nothing looked familiar. I looked down at the speedometer and I was still coasting along at almost seventy miles per hour. When I glanced at the exit sign coming up, I realized I was several miles further down the road from where I blacked out.

That repeat occurrence of my Haiti healing while blinded was a sign for me that it was a true miracle and not the result of medicine. I remember saying over and over as I drove the rest of the way home, "Thank you, God. I will never doubt You again." Yes, God is real.

Chapter 11
MAGIC MONEY

Even though I didn't suffer from any more ulcers, I had no desire to go back to the corporate world. However, I still didn't know what serving God was supposed to mean, so I started by doing what I enjoyed the most.

I owned every Sears Craftsman tool on Earth, had good carpentry skills, and architectural drafting experience. I started my own home improvement company. Actually, that was just a fancy title to save face and look important when I handed out my business card. All I really did initially was small home repairs. My way to serve God was to do these repairs as cheaply as possible, so that it would be a blessing to my customers. Opposite the norm, my goal was to make as little profit as necessary to keep the business going. My intention was to help someone who otherwise couldn't afford to have the work done, and if I'm going to be completely honest, it would also be a good tax write-off. I named the business Christian Works, and I usually did two or three small jobs in the same day around the small town of Pacific, Missouri, about forty miles west of St. Louis.

Due to the nature of the repairs, they were mostly labor and few materials, so I didn't need to carry much cash around with me. I charged people by the hour, and they paid me before I left them. The rate customers paid me was negotiable. I would work for a poor widow for five dollars an hour; a family with sufficient income would pay me around fifteen dollars and hour; and a doctor or lawyer would give me thirty-five to fifty dollars. I let the customers help decide how much they could afford to pay me.

After one of the first jobs I did, I noticed I had too much money in my wallet. I figured a customer must have overpaid me, but after a couple more jobs, I noticed the same thing seemed to be happening. When I did my accounting ledger at the end of each day, I kept ending up with more money than I charged the customers for. I thought, "I used to be a corporate executive keeping track of millions of dollars, and now I can't even keep track of a few bucks?" I tracked the next day more closely and kept a good eye on what I paid out for materials and what the customers paid me, but somewhere I was making a mistake. I kept ending up with more money than I should have had.

I decided that was it. The next day I had several jobs to do, so I kept all the receipts and stapled them to the proper invoices for each job. I made sure there was no other money in my wallet, and I knew I had done my bookwork properly.

That night I went down to my office in our basement to file all the paperwork away. I pulled out my wallet to recount it one last time, and there was a ton of extra cash in it. I mean a lot of extra cash. The only reason I could come up with was that maybe someone that day gave me the wrong change back, handing me a bunch of ten-dollar bills instead of one-dollar bills.

I was starting to suspect I might be in the twilight zone, so I decided to run the situation by Melainie. She listened, didn't make fun of me, and said, "Well, let's just see what happens." Together we stood at the dresser in our bedroom and carefully put only one twenty-dollar bill in my wallet for the next day.

I only had one customer scheduled for that day. All I had to do was replace some broken window glass in a small trailer, so I knew twenty dollars would be enough money. The customer was a woman with three kids who was down on her luck after her husband had left her. It was cold, starting to snow, and when I go to the customer's home, the snowflakes were blowing in the windows where two whole panes of glass were missing. I ran to the local hardware store and got the glass cut to the sizes I needed. It was only $5.60, so I put the change of fourteen dollars back in my wallet and the forty cents in my pocket.

It took several hours to get this job done because I fixed a few other things for her while I was there, little things like realigning the strike-plate on the front-door lock and adjusting the back door threshold so the door wouldn't stick shut.

When it came time to collect my fee for the repairs, I sat down at her kitchen table, which was also falling apart, and began to write her an invoice. As I wrote it, I looked around her trailer and saw the terrible conditions she and her children had to live in. My heart broke. I couldn't dare charge her for anything. She asked me how much she owed me and I told her she didn't owe me a dime. She thanked me, but she was too embarrassed to look me in the face.

I went straight home from that job and got undressed to take a shower. I pulled my wallet out and threw it on the dresser. Melainie and I had made a deal to check it together this time.

When she got home from work, I filled her in on all the details of the job, including the fourteen dollars in bills that was left in my wallet. I told her this wasn't going to be a good test because I didn't have the heart to take any money from the woman. Still, I had the receipt for the glass, so we went upstairs to the bedroom and opened the wallet together. We found twenty-one dollars in my wallet. All I can remember Melainie saying to me was her usual comment, "Humph."

Looking at each other, we hesitated in silence. In our minds we were thinking of possible explanations for this, but we both knew better. As soon as I started to mention some possibilities, a chill ran through my stomach, and I remembered the blackout in the car when I promised never to doubt God again. We both knew this was no coincidence or mistake. This was God.

I know a seven dollar increase seems a little hokey for a supernatural testimony, but it was the beginning of even greater miracles that God did with our finances.

Chapter 12

WHO'S THERE?

MELAINIE GOT MORE INVOLVED WITH METH-odist history and doctrines until she wanted to go away on a three-day retreat called the Walk to Emmaus. This was supposed to be an ecumenical study of Christ, where people from different denominations gather together to share the similarities in their beliefs, not their differences.

The walk was designed for couples so that men go first and two weeks later their spouses go through the same program. When I questioned our pastor about the program, I found out that it was secretive—they couldn't tell me about it before I went or it would supposedly ruin the effect of the program.

I had heard that kind of sales pitch before. It sounded like a brainwashing trick to me, so I didn't want any part of it, even if it was a church function.

Melainie was not eligible to go if I didn't go, which just convinced me all the more that there was something not quite right about this program. I absolutely refused to participate, but Melainie was so determined that she had our pastor write a letter of petition to allow her to attend the walk without my participation. Their program board consented, and Melainie was gone, doing something secretive.

When she returned home from the walk, she told me little bits and pieces, but kept quiet about most of it. I would have been worried about this secretive stuff if it weren't for the big change I noticed in her personality. This hard woman was now a softer, more compassionate person. She was still a gung-ho Methodist, but now she had a peace and a contentment that wasn't there before.

While Melainie was getting more entrenched in the Methodist church, I was drawing away from it. In fact, I was drawing away from all church denominations. The more I read the Bible, the more it seemed denominations were separating people instead of uniting them. But Melainie didn't give up on me. For three years she tried to convince me that going on the walk would enrich my relationship with God, and for those three years, she seemed to know a lot more about God than I did.

Ever since the Walk to Emmaus retreat, she had been quoting a scripture to me, John 8:32: "Know the truth, and the truth will set you free." I thought I was free, because I felt free to do whatever I wanted, whenever I wanted to do it. I didn't yet realize there was a difference between being free in the natural, earthly things, and being free in the supernatural, or spiritual things. She repeated that verse to me at every opportunity, even though she knew I didn't understand exactly what she was trying to convey to me.

Melainie would always get up at the wee hours of the

morning (4:00 a.m.) to study and pray before she went to work. She had a study area on the balcony right outside our bedroom. She would always be quiet so as not to disturb my sleep, but one morning I could hear her singing. Now this really bothered me. She was getting so close to God she was actually singing songs to Him? I was astounded, so I listened closely. When she finished singing that morning, she came back into the bedroom, pulled the covers down, and crawled back into bed instead of getting dressed for work. I remember feeling the bed sag and the covers move as she pressed her back up against me the way we normally slept.

This time when she pressed up to me, though, I felt that same warm, oozy feeling that I've mentioned many times before. Neither one of us said a word, and after laying there barely a minute, she pulled the covers off and started to get back up. I rolled over quickly and tried to grab her to kiss her good-bye, but she wasn't there. I called out, "Melainie?" but there was no answer. The whole house was dark. I looked at the clock and realized she had left for work quite some time ago.

Not long after that, Melainie's singing woke me up again. I didn't recognize the song, but it was so comforting I just kept lying there as that same feeling started flowing again. That feeling fled the instant I thought I heard a distressed call from her. I heard her call my name, but it was a deeper voice, as if she were sick or crying. When she called again, I knew something was wrong, so I hollered back: "What?" She didn't answer, so I jumped up and rushed out to the balcony shouting, "What's the matter?" I didn't see her, so I ran down the stairs. I kept calling, "What do you want?" but she was nowhere in sight. I opened the garage door to see if she was outside, and I saw that her car was gone.

Standing in the doorway, I stopped to think and realized once again that Melainie was already at work. I felt that warmth all over my body like a shower, and I just stood there for a while, stunned. I had heard stories before, just like you have, of God calling somebody by name. I knew it was in the Bible, too. But I thought they heard it in the Spirit, like when the Holy Spirit imparted knowledge to me in the past. I didn't believe that I could hear God in a real, audible voice, and if this was God, how could I get His voice confused with Melainie's voice? It didn't sound like a man's voice, but then again, it didn't sound like a woman's voice either.

Several weeks later I was in a dead, sound sleep when I was awakened by a call from that same voice again. This time I heard it speak firmly, "Roy." I opened my eyes and looked around the room to see if anyone was there. It was daylight, and Melainie was gone. When the voice called my name a second time, I was determined to find out if this was really happening to me or if I was just dreaming. I was wide awake and staring at the ceiling. I didn't move a muscle, except to ask out loud, "God, is this You?" Immediately I heard back, "I am here. Where are you?" Then there was nothing but silence.

I was so shocked by hearing an answer that my body felt like it was being pricked all over with pins and needles. I stayed perfectly still for a long time, but I heard nothing more. I couldn't answer back because I didn't understand the question. Where are you? I thought, "If this is God, how could He not know where I am? Where am I? I'm in bed." I kept thinking of my location, but that wasn't what God was asking me. The familiar feeling of God's Spirit was replaced by a cold, empty feeling, like a bottomless pit.

So, where was I? I was perplexed over that question for several weeks. It took that long for me to realize I was still getting drunk once in a while. I was still watching nasty movies on TV. I was still telling dirty jokes and cursing. I was still cheating on my taxes. I was still doing all those things and thinking it was okay with God. That is what God meant when He asked me, "Where are you?" The word *sin* was too old-fashioned for me. I didn't consider the things I was doing to be sins; they seemed to be normal things that everybody else did, too. I hadn't thought sins could really separate us from God, because I knew God would forgive us and let us in to heaven. From that experience on, however, I realized those actions weren't acceptable and that they were keeping me from receiving the blessings of God.

Weeks later, something woke me up in the middle of the night. There were no voices or dreams this time. I just woke up. I went downstairs, opened the refrigerator, took out a bottle of wine, walked outside to the trashcan, and threw the bottle in it. Then I went back to bed and right back to sleep.

A few nights after that, the same thing happened again. I just abruptly woke up, unlocked a drawer next to the bed and pulled out a sleazy, X-rated bachelor party video, walked outside to the trash can, and threw the video in it. Like before, I went straight back to bed and right back to sleep as if nothing had happened.

But something had happened. From then on I didn't

get drunk anymore, nudity in movies embarrassed me, it actually hurt me to hear profane words, dirty jokes weren't funny anymore, and I couldn't claim one-tenth of a mile on my tax deductions that wasn't accurate or honest.

I was set free, just like it said in the verse Melainie had quoted to me so many times.

My curiosity over the change and wisdom in my wife after the Walk to Emmaus finally got the best of me, so I finally went to that three-day retreat to see if it would do as much for me as it had done for her. And guess what? The secret stuff that I was so apprehensive about turned out to be a most heart-warming experience. They were right. Some of the events would have been more meaningful if Melainie had kept them a secret and not shared details with me over the years.

The Walk helped me find the missing link that had been limiting my search for God. At the Walk, God revealed to me that Melainie was not just my wife, but she was also my equal in Christ. I finally received the freedom not only to pray in unity with my wife, but I also experienced the desire to do so for the first time. At the time I had no idea how great of an effect our combined prayers would have on the course of both our lives.

Chapter 13
DOCUMENTED, UNDENIABLE PROOF

E VERYTHING WAS GOING GREAT FOR US—WITH one, humongous exception. For two years I had been telling everyone about my ulcer healing in Haiti, and I hadn't had a single problem with my stomach during those two years. There were no ulcers, no bleeding, no stomach attacks for two full years. I even wrote a testimony about it and gave more than 1,500 copies out to people. Then, suddenly, in 1986 the same kind of pain and bleeding I had experienced from those ulcers was back.

For a few weeks, I was devastated, but not because of the pain and bleeding. The way I saw it, if those symptoms had returned, then the ulcers had come back, which to many people would mean that I had never been healed in the first place. I agonized over the thought that everyone who heard or read my testimony would lose faith in miracles and healing because of me. What was I supposed to say to people after the ulcers were back?

I concealed the stomach problems I was having for a little while, hoping it would just go away and I would never have to tell anyone about the reoccurrence. Soon, however, I had to wake Melainie up one night because the pain in my stomach was so severe I couldn't breathe. She helped me into the car and we headed for St. Anthony's Hospital.

As she was driving, I was grumbling because I didn't understand why God would let this happen to me again. She was praying quietly at first, sort of under her breath. When she started praying out loud, I reached over, grabbed her right hand, and pushed it up against my stomach. For the next four or five miles, Melainie prayed and drove with one hand on the steering wheel and one hand on my stomach. We were almost at the hospital when I asked her to pull the car over to the side of the road. Praying together was still a fairly new thing for me, so when she prayed for me like that, I was a little embarrassed that I couldn't handle the situation all by myself.

When the car stopped, I got out without saying a word to her and walked around for a few minutes. I wanted to move around and wait to make sure I wasn't imagining anything. While her hand was on my stomach, I got relief from the pain. It was a slow relief. I could feel the pain getting numb, like it was dissolving away. I got back in the car and told Melainie the pain had stopped. She looked at me with a smirk on her face, and all she said was, "So, are we still going to the hospital, or should I turn around?" Still dazed and not sure what to make of it, I replied, "Uh, I think we can go home now." On the way home, I felt that warm, oozy feeling flowing over me again, only this time I was really light-headed. I felt like I was drunk.

I was humbled. There I was, the head of the household and the supposed spiritual leader of the family, and it was clear that God was really working through Melainie. I couldn't fathom how she had prayed for me with one hand and the pain went away.

Melainie's prayer saved me that night on the way to the hospital, but over time the pain and bleeding became constant and got even worse. I was going to have to confess that my ulcer problem was back. Before I broke the news to everyone that my healing didn't last, I returned to Dr. John Eckrich for more ulcer treatments. He scheduled another endoscopy to see how bad the ulcers were this time, and guess what? The camera showed that there were no ulcers at all. In fact, there wasn't even any scar tissue left from where the ulcers had previously been before. Now this was the very same doctor who had told me that even if they were able to heal all of my ulcers, I would live with scar tissue in my stomach for the rest of my life. After Dr. Eckrich told me that I didn't have any scar tissue, I asked him how those scars could disappear. He just shook his head. When I briefly shared the testimony of my healing in Haiti with him, he replied, "This is very unusual, but there are lots of documented healings like yours on file that the medical sciences can't really explain." Dr. Eckrich still didn't know what was causing the pain and bleeding, but at least I didn't have to retract the testimony of my healing from the ulcers!

Many years later a St. Louis newspaper, the *Riverfront Times*, interviewed me for a story they were doing on healings and miracles. From the nature of that newspaper, I figured they wanted to discredit my testimony and say that my ulcer healing was only my word, and that such a thing never really happened. After an extensive phone interview, I submitted to them all the hospital medical records and the appropriate reports to verify my ulcer healing with documented, undeniable proof. There were the written, signed, and sworn details by the professionals that the permanent scarring condition from the ulcers that was to have existed in my stomach forever had totally disappeared.

To my surprise, when the article came out the newspaper did not distort the facts or misrepresent any of the information. They reported the evidence and proof of my healing, though they didn't call it a miracle. Instead, they said it was "unexplainable."

After fourteen years of marriage and still no children, we adopted a two-year-old boy from Madras, India, named baby Emmanuel. The Christian organization we went through, Love Basket Inc., took care of everything so we didn't have to travel to India. We just had to choose which child to adopt. When you have a natural birth, you don't have any choice over who your child is or what he or she looks like, but when you adopt, you actually have to pick a human life. It's tough. The hardest part isn't selecting one; it's knowing that you're leaving behind all the ones you didn't choose. Melainie and

I found our hearts aching with the thought of what would become of the ones we didn't pick.

We kept Emmanuel as our son's middle name and gave him the first name Derek. With his jet-black hair and dark skin, we didn't want a less common name to cause him unwanted attention or teasing from other kids.

It wasn't until I had my own son that I understood the depth of what God did to save us. There is no way I could allow anyone to torture and hang my son on a cross. They would have to hang me first!

Melainie stayed on with Southwestern Bell and I played "Mr. Mom" for a few years. I continued operating Christian Works from home, so that gave me plenty of time to do the daily household chores and slip away occasionally on more volunteer mission trips.

No matter how many times I was tested or hospitalized for a stomach attack, the doctors never could determine what caused them. By 1992, the pain was so severe it would cause me to hyperventilate. All the hospital emergency rooms could do was to give me a shot of Demerol, a strong pain medication, to get me through the night.

The bleeding became daily and was so heavy I got light-headed if I stood up quickly. Melainie said my skin color used to look as white as a bed sheet at times. Since they never found the source of the bleeding, all the doctors could do was comfort me with these not-so-comforting words: "Yes, Mr. Davidson, you do have internal bleeding. No, we can't tell you where it is coming from, but don't worry. If it were going to kill you, it would have done so by now."

The pain of these attacks was so bad I couldn't bear the thought of having to go through another night of rolling on the floor. It felt like a pressure, like some very sensitive internal organ was being squeezed or crushed. It was a constant, steady pain that never let up during the sixteen-hour attacks. I never had the thought of doing something drastic to myself, but because of these attacks I do understand why some people take their own life rather than endure chronic pain.

That same year I was in a car accident that left me with an injury that limited the upward motion of my neck. Two years later, I was still having difficulty with pain in my neck when lying down or working with my head tilted back. When it came time to paint the exterior of my house, I didn't even give it a second thought. I always painted it myself because it was so big and would cost way more than I wanted to pay someone else to do it. It was a frame house with hardboard siding and sat on an elevation that made it necessary to use a forty-foot ladder to reach the back side. There was so much to paint and trim that it took many weeks to finish it all.

The first time I climbed up the ladder and leaned my head back to look up at the soffit, my neck locked and I couldn't move. The slightest movement sent shooting pains down my back and legs. I couldn't even twitch a finger without sending a paralyzing pain through my body. Rung by painstaking rung, it took a long time to make my way down the ladder.

Once I was back on the ground, I stood there for a minute and started to pray. My prayer was more like a demand than a plea. I said, "God, I have got to get this work done. I don't want to pay someone else to do what I can do myself. You have to take this pain away and fix my neck so I can paint my house." Instantly, the pain left my neck. I went right back up the ladder and painted every day, all summer long, and much of it with my head tilted back.

It still didn't make sense to me why God would heal my ulcers and neck pain but not the stomach attacks, but I decided to continue believing that He would take care of me.

Chapter 14
HEAVY DEMONS

It wasn't long before Melainie and I learned that if you're going to stick your neck out there and trust God, then you had better be ready to handle the tough stuff, too. If you're going to take a stand that God is real, you had better be ready to accept the truth that demons are real also. We all like to think about angels being real because they are good, but not many people want to believe the devil or demons are real. In the movies, demons and demonic activity is portrayed as too sensational or science-fictional to seem real to most people. It's easier for people to believe in outer space creatures than to believe demons are real.

The truth, my friend, is that you can feel and see the presence of an evil spirit, just like you can feel and see the presence of an angelic one. The supernatural powers of evil are just as real as the supernatural powers of God. Just watch any report about Jeffrey Dahmer or other such criminals. If you think people who can do that are just mentally insane and not demon possessed, then you are kidding yourself.

I've heard some great testimonies from reputable people who have had visions or encounters with angels. Though I haven't seen an angel myself, my wife and I have seen supernatural manifestations with our physical eyes. After Melainie came back from the Walk to Emmaus, she would describe seeing certain people light up like a bright, white glow whenever she felt the strong presence of God around them. The first time this happened to her was at our Methodist church when our friend, Jim, was standing at the pulpit reading a scripture. Later, it began occurring in places other than the church. She would always tell me when it was happening, but I never saw anything. Since her "light-people," as she called them, never had any significant meaning or purpose to me, I didn't give them any thought. That is, until it happened to me.

It was only one time, but while Pastor Rick Shelton was preaching at Life Christian Center one Sunday, I saw a bright, white light surround him. It was not a ball of light, like a spotlight. Instead, I saw a band of light about twelve inches wide that followed the whole contour of his body, as if you drew an outline around him. On the outer edge of that white light was a brilliant purple color only about three or four inches wide.

I leaned over to Melainie and asked: "Do you see that?" She said, "See what?" When I described to her what I was seeing, she just smiled at me and said, "Oh, so you can see my light-people, too." For several minutes as Pastor Rick preached and moved around on the pulpit, the light stayed right in place around him, moving just like he did. I had no idea what it was about. I have no revelation or explanation for it at all. My guess is God was confirming for me that Melainie really was seeing such visions and preparing me for supernatural sights yet to come.

After Melainie and I started praying together and became more in one accord in our efforts to know and serve God, we began to experience the attacks of evil powers.

Not long after we began our prayer times together, Melainie was intensely studying everything she could get her hands on, while I kept listening to my same old twelve cassette tapes over and over again. Melainie brought home a book someone at work had loaned her about the essence of human evil. The book explained how Satan uses lies to control humans and how that bondage can only be overcome through confrontation and Christian love. When I asked her why she wanted to read something like that, she replied that Christians need to know how Satan works. I had already begun listening to a new tape on spiritual warfare by Pat Robertson, and I knew it wasn't any coincidence that we both ended up doing a study on evil spirits at the same time.

Not long after we began that study, our family went to bed after an ordinary weeknight. Derek and Melainie were very sound sleepers. On the other hand, I was such a light sleeper that from our bedroom I could hear the rustle of Derek's covers as he turned over in his bed—down the hall. Around 2:00 a.m., I woke slowly to what sounded like someone calling Melainie's name. I didn't wake up all at once, but I knew I had to wake myself up completely to see if it was Derek who was calling.

As I got more alert, I could tell it wasn't Derek. Instead, the voice was deep and raspy. It just kept calling my wife's name: "Melainie…Melainie." I turned over on my back and thought I saw a dark shadow move in the room. I cleared my eyes, and it looked like there was some dark shape or shadow blocking the doorway. I sat up in bed to try to figure out what I was looking at and dropped my jaw with surprise. What I saw shocked me wide-awake. Standing on Melainie's side of the room near the foot of our bed was a black, hooded figure, shaped like a person. I couldn't see a face or any arms, and there was an awful, heavy, weighty feeling pressing on me. This thing didn't seem to acknowledge me at all. It just kept calling, "Melainie."

I looked down at Melainie, who was still sound asleep. She hadn't heard a thing. I reached over and shook her to wake her up. When I saw her eyes open, I asked her, "Do you see that?" She didn't answer, but she jolted straight up in bed right next to me.

Once she was sitting up, this dark figure started talking to us. It kept repeating the same phrase over and over, "Melainie, you're going the wrong way." It didn't say anything else, and we certainly didn't talk back to it. The awful, abysmal feeling this demon emitted was really frightening.

As the demon kept repeating that phrase, we looked at each other, grabbed each others' hands, and by pure instinct we both began to pray out loud to rebuke this demon and demand that it leave us alone. We prayed louder and louder, almost shouting, to drown out what the demon was saying, and we prayed for a hedge of protection around Derek. We knew from our studies that to defeat demonic spirits, we had to pray in the name of Jesus, so we did. While we were praying, the demon just disappeared, right before our eyes.

What do you think Melainie and I did then? After such a traumatic experience, you would think we'd be pretty shaken and disturbed, wouldn't you? Actually, we didn't say a word to each other. We didn't even get out of bed to go check on Derek. We both laid straight back down and went back to sleep like nothing had happened. When something this supernatural happens to you, you are not normal. When the power of God comes over you, you can't think, act, or be normal. You are in a state of protection, or anointing, that takes over, and you don't function like normal until that anointing lifts.

The next morning we talked about the experience plenty. We compared notes to the infinite detail and confirmed that we both saw and heard the exact same thing. This was the most ghastly thing that had happened in our lives so far. Since the demon specifically called Melainie by name, we contributed the visitation to the book that only she had been reading. I know the title and author of the book, but I won't tell you. I don't want you to look for a copy of it to read and put yourself or your family at risk. It's strange how demons work and can attach themselves to people. Bringing that book into our home was like opening a door and broadcasting, "Demons, come and get us!" I should have made Melainie burn that book, but I only insisted that she return it, and return it immediately!

Many years later, in 1998, I went on a mission trip with Habitat for Humanity to help build houses in Uganda, East Africa. After the mission was over and we were preparing to return to the United States, my heart sunk with an overwhelming burden over the appalling, impoverished conditions many of the Ugandan people live in.

I paced up and down a red clay road the night before we left Uganda, and I had another one of my discussions with God. It went like this: "God, I don't understand this. How can I go home to my nice house with running water and plenty of food, while these people are going to live and die, sleeping on the dirt? This is not right. You have got to make some sense out of this for me." I knew I couldn't go home and return to living the American life of luxury with the thought that two-thirds of the people in the world still sleep on the ground under a thatched roof, while they suffered such hardships.

On the way home, our plane had a layover for several hours in Brussels, Belgium. During those hours I got to the point of no return. I actually put my foot down with God and told Him, "God, I am not going home. I am going to spend time alone with You until You make some sense of this for me." I called Melainie and woke her up in the middle of the night to inform her that I wasn't coming home until I spent some time alone with God. I explained that I was going back to my favorite place in the entire world, Egypt, and that I would not be in contact with her or anyone else for the next two weeks. All she could say to me was, "Well, if you know what you've got do, I guess you've got to do it. Who am I to tell you, you can't go follow God?"

Whenever I went on a mission trip, I would always give all my clothes and money to people instead of bringing anything back home with me. Such was the case this time. So all by myself, with almost no money and only the clothes I was wearing, I took off for a two-week trek through the deserts of Egypt. I was determined to totally trust and rely on God and God only for everything. Wherever I went, whatever I ate, and whatever I did, I was going to follow God and try to pray unceasingly the whole time.

With no interpreter, I traveled around, stopping from place to place and having all my basic needs met. I ended up going to some of the historic and religious centers of ancient times all the while getting the revelations I needed from God.

Finding places to sleep with little money was a bit challenging. In Egypt it is common for hotel entrances to be located on the second or third floors of buildings, instead of on the street level. To get a room, you have to go in narrow doorways and walk up two or three flights of stairs before you get to a small hotel lobby. Most of the stairwells are dimly lit, and often there are shady looking characters hanging around inside. Walking in these places alone was kind of tense.

Arriving in Old Cairo about three o'clock one morning, a cab driver dropped me off in front of a hotel entrance. I thanked him, grabbed my small suitcase, and started up the stairs out of his sight. Before he drove off, he noticed a rough-looking local come out of the shadows and scurry in behind me. When I reached the second floor, it was a dead end. To get to the lobby, I was going to have to get in a one-man elevator that was less than two feet square. As I stepped into it, I realized I wouldn't have enough room to turn around. I started to step out of the elevator to turn around and back into it, but it was too late. Before I finished figuring out what to do, a hard shove came from behind and I found myself pinned face-first up against the wall in that tiny space. I couldn't budge an inch.

The man pushed me in with his back, while he braced his feet up against the sides of the door opening to keep me crushed against the wall. I was in big trouble. I kept trying to scream for help while he kept screaming something in Arabic, but no one was within hearing distance. I was expecting to feel a knife in my side at any moment. I had to act fast, and as quick as that thought flashed in my mind, I froze. Yep, as soon as my adrenaline kicked in and I was ready to kill or be killed, I found myself praying. I melted like a marshmallow and went limp as I thought, "God, I don't want to hurt this man."

Can you believe that? There was no telling what this guy was going to do to me, and I froze, just like people do in the movies. It was just as that thought came into my mind that my cab driver appeared in the stairwell and began to wrestle me free from my attacker. He had been suspicious of the way the guy sneaked in behind me, so he parked the cab, flew up the stairs, and came to my aid. We scuffled all the way back down to the street, where I smashed the guy's hand in the door of the cab in order to get away from him. We drove off with the guy on his knees in the middle of the street bellowing out in pain.

As we sped down the road, the cab driver said, "Don't worry. I know good hotel." But it didn't matter. My conscience started eating me up. I couldn't drive away and leave the man injured in the street alone. I told the driver to turn around. "We have to go back and help that guy," I said. The cab driver swung his head around in astonishment. "What?" he asked. I told him again that we needed to go back and make sure the man was OK. The driver looked at me as if I were from the moon and shook his head while explaining that it was not a good idea. Nonetheless, I finally convinced him to drive back to the scene.

It took a few minutes to get there, and as we approached the hotel, we could see there were now three people in the street: the guy who attacked me and two police officers. My attacker was laid out face down, quiet, and not moving. One of the policemen had apparently cold-cocked him with the billy club in his hand. The driver slowed the cab down to a crawl and asked me if we should stop. I said, "No, I think he's in good hands now. Where's this other hotel?"

In nineteen years of traveling abroad alone, this was the only confrontation I ever had with another person, but that was not the case when it came to confrontations with something other than human.

Another night it was getting late, and I needed to get in off the streets before it got too dark. I had just arrived in the small town of Luxor, built on the location of the ancient city of Thebes. There were other places to stay in this town, but since I was trying to follow God's guidance, it seemed like a room above a certain café was the right place, especially since it was only a dollar a night.

The café building was at the far end of a dead-end street with some rough-looking men hanging around outside. It was a second-story room with no glass in the windows, only one narrow stairway to get in and out, no lights, and the door handle had been ripped off (several times, from the looks of it), leaving no latch to keep the door closed. I usually felt secure at night once I found a room, but in this place I felt uneasy after bunking down. Lying in a rickety, old, musty bed, my mind started to run away with thoughts of what could happen to me in a place like that. The unkempt Egyptian men hanging around outside in their dirty gowns and ragged turbans looked far from friendly, and it was so dark in my room I couldn't see my hand in front of my face.

Being as street-smart as I was, I got up and shoved a huge dresser in front of the door so no one could sneak in while I was sleeping. When I got back in bed and gave a sigh of relief, God started slapping me in the head with this question: Good grief, Roy, are you going to trust Me to keep you safe, or are you going to trust a dresser? With that revelation, I felt foolish for barricading the door, but not foolish enough to get up and move it away. The next day I was comforted by that revelation about God's intent to protect me, but I went off to find a better, safer room to stay in anyway. I did this on my own without praying or asking God first.

Nearby was a clean, almost brand-new boardinghouse. It had glass in the windows, a door with a lock, electric lights, and a guard in the entrance all night. I took it. At three dollars a night, it was way more than I should have paid, but for the security, it was worth it. That night I got undressed, locked the door, and crawled into a strong, well-built wood bed. Even with my room light off, I could see everything easily. Light came in from the hallway under the door and through a small gap around the perimeter of the door.

Being a light sleeper, every little noise in the hall woke me up during the night. I was trying to get back to sleep when my chest started hurting me. I was lying on my back looking straight at the door when I saw smoke beginning to creep in around the gap. My first thought was that there must have been a fire and I had been inhaling some fumes. It felt like a heavy lead weight had been placed on my chest, and it was making it difficult to breathe. The pressure got heavier and heavier. Then it felt like somebody wrapped their hands or tied a noose around my throat. The smoke started to form together and take on a shape, so I knew what was happening. It wasn't the same demonic shape Melainie and I had seen at home, but it was similar.

By the time it came together in its regular shape, I could barely breathe from the pressure on my chest and the tightness around my throat. It felt like somebody parked a car on top of me. I couldn't raise my arms or move a muscle, much less get up out of bed. I began praying, but I couldn't pray out loud. No matter how hard I tried, I couldn't get enough breath to make an audible sound. It was dreadful. I thought I was going to suffocate. The ghastly presence of evil coming from this demon was so strong that I panicked, thinking the thing was going to kill me.

I could see straight through the demon to the door

the whole time this was happening. It moved around like a dark but transparent cloud of smoke that could change form. It didn't have any hands or face. I saw the demon reform and attach itself to both of my legs at my shins, causing an intense pain on them. The demon pressed down harder and harder until I heard a loud cracking sound like the bed, or my legs, were breaking. It hurt so bad, I knew it had to be my legs.

I thought this was the end. I knew I had to cry out then, or it would be too late. With everything I could muster up inside me, I barely squeezed one word out of my mouth. It was so soft and muffled you could hardly hear it. All I could get out was the name of Jesus.

The second I said "Jesus," the attack was over. The pain and pressure went away, and I could breathe. I stayed there in bed shaking and trembling with fear as the demon dissipated and drifted back out the gap in the door. I don't remember getting back to sleep that night, but I do remember lying there, apologizing to God over and over. I promised Him I'd never let my physical environment or situation undermine my complete trust in Him again. I was safer in that rickety café room that God led me to than I was in the place that I thought looked safe. From that night on, when I say, "God will take care of me," I mean it, without any reservations.

One last note: when I got up to get dressed the next morning, I sat on the edge of the bed and leaned down to pick up my socks. As I leaned forward, I could see under the bed. There were only three slats that held the whole mattress up in place. The one slat that was right under where my shins were as I laid in bed was broken out and lying on the floor.

Demons are real, and their purpose is to separate you from God. Looking back, I now believe that attack on me was to take my life and thus prevent me from writing this book and telling you the testimonies that you are going to be reading on the pages to come.

Chapter 15
UNHOLY YACHT

A BIG PART OF OUR LIFE WAS THE SIXTEEN YEARS we spent pleasure boating. The Lake of the Ozarks was only a couple hours drive from home for us, so Melainie and I were into the fun-in-the-sun lifestyle in a big way. This lifestyle kept getting bigger and bigger, until our sixth boat grew into a ten-meter Trojan yacht.

I admit we bought it for comfort and convenience, but we did have an ulterior motive. We wanted to provide a place where our friends could swim, eat, and sleep at no expense. We knew a lot of people who couldn't afford a summer vacation if they had to pay for it themselves, so we wanted to have a big enough boat that others could live on it with us for a weekend.

A tradition in boating is to name your vessel in a way that reflects something special in your life. We appropriately named our boat *Witness* and included the Christian fish symbol in the name. The beam, or width of the boat, was thirteen feet, so once the name was painted in huge block letters across the stern (that's the rear end for you non-boaters), it kind of looked like a floating billboard from behind. You couldn't miss it.

Witness was a brand-new boat, but being a display model at the marina, salesmen had used it extensively for partying before we bought it. After we took possession, we found clothing and some other items hidden onboard that made us suspicious about the kind of parties they had. Once we made that discovery, we had an uneasy feeling about the boat. Sure enough, on several occasions while sleeping on the *Witness*, I would wake up during the night feeling a heavy presence or having a bad dream. I'd wake Melainie and we'd pray together until the heavy presence went away. We never got a handle on what the presence was, nor did we ever see or hear any manifestations of anything. It just felt bad.

Our boating season in the Midwest was approximately May to October, so at the close of each season, I would go to the lake and stay on the boat by myself while I winterized it from freezing temperatures. There were lots of fluids to drain and anti-freeze solutions to install, as well as the normal cleaning and waxing. To get all of that done, I typically stayed there two or three nights.

In the fall of 1990, I started winterizing by cleaning all the towels, blankets, and bed linens and stowing them away for the next season. I took along a sleeping bag to keep from using any of the clean linens once they were stowed.

Since I was alone, I decided to sleep in the forward V-berth instead of the mid-cabin, where Melainie and I always slept together. Being a guy with no one there to see what I was doing, I did the lazy man's thing and slept in my clothes. I was sleeping great, right under the bow hatch, when the feeling of something wet woke me up. The back of my shirt was so wet it was stuck to my skin. My first thought was that it must have been raining and the hatch was open or leaking.

I sat up and looked out the hatch to discover it was a clear, dry night. Then it felt like there was water running down my back. I stuck my hand down the back of my shirt, and when I pulled my hand out, it was soaking wet. When I brought it back in front of my face, I saw that it was covered with blood. I looked down at the sleeping bag to see that it was drenched with blood. While I was looking at the sleeping bag, I felt that same heavy presence that Melainie and I had felt on the boat before. I didn't see or hear anything, but I sprang to my feet and began praying against evil spirits. I stayed in one spot with my eyes closed and hands folded. I don't remember what I prayed or how long, but I stopped praying and opened my eyes as soon as the heavy presence went away.

I looked down at the bed and saw that I had a real mess to clean up. I took my shirt off and rolled it up in the sleeping bag. I laid the sleeping bag on the floor in the bathroom and began washing my hands and my back. I couldn't believe how much blood was on me. As I wiped it off, it splattered on the faucet, the counter, and even on the cabinet doors. Since the bath towels were already stowed, I used some of our special winterizing towels for cleaning up the blood. It took two or three of them to wipe myself and the sink down. I threw the towels on top of the sleeping bag. They were white towels, and they were going to need plenty of bleach to get rid of all the bloodstains on them.

There was a big mirror on the wall alongside the bathroom sink. I started examining my back for a cut, but I couldn't even find a scratch. There were no marks or signs of anything on my back. There was no reason for the blood.

It was getting close to daylight, so I opened my duffel bag and put on a clean shirt. I pulled a blanket out of the linen closet, checked to make sure the mattress was clean and dry, and flopped down on the bed to ponder what had just happened. I didn't even try to go back to sleep. I just kept quizzing God about what this meant. Was it some kind of a sign, or did it have something to do with my internal bleeding? I thought and listened for God till the sun came up, but I didn't get any understanding on this.

As soon as it was light enough outside, I got back up to take all the bloody stuff to the laundry mat. I wanted to get there as early as possible so nobody else would be there to see the mess and think I was a mass murderer or something. I walked back to the bathroom to get the sleeping bag and towels, and when I picked them up in my hands and examined them, they were all clean and dry. There was no trace of blood anywhere.

So, what was that all about? To this day I have no idea. All I know is that it happened. Many things have occurred in my life that I didn't get an understanding or revelation on until years later. This is one of those things. Maybe God will explain this to me someday, and maybe not.

A year later I was in St. Louis inquiring about some sewing repairs for a canvas Bimini top. Like Pop used to do, I managed to drop a mention of God into the conversation I was having with one of the employees there. As I was inviting the employee to visit my church, he got really excited and said, "Oh, I already belong to a church. You should have heard our pastor's sermon last week. He wrote a whole sermon about some big boat he saw down at the Lake of the Ozarks named *Witness*."

I told the guy that was my boat, but I don't think he believed me. It didn't matter whether he believed me or not, because I was too excited by the news that our boat may have had the effect on others that Melainie and I had been praying for.

In 1992 we sold the *Witness* to a crude, abrasive guy needing a tax shelter for his computer business. After the deal was done and Melainie and I were walking away, the guy called out to us, "Hey, I've been meaning to ask you: what does *Witness* mean, anyway? And what kind of symbol is that?" After I explained it to him he said, "Oh, so it's a religious thing. I thought you were some kind of a lawyer." Melainie grabbed my arm tightly and whispered softly, "That poor guy. If he doesn't know God and he's buying that boat—with whatever spirit has been hanging around on it—he's in for some real trouble!"

Chapter 16
I'M A WHAT?

I TOLD YOU THAT MELAINIE AND I WERE NOW PRAYING and studying together, and we were becoming more in one accord with God. But that didn't mean we were always on the same page together. When Melainie decided she would enroll as a candidate for ordained ministry, I definitely was not on that page.

She wanted to officially become a Methodist minister, and I questioned her motives. She certainly wanted to serve God, but why did she want to be a Methodist? Why not a Lutheran, or a Baptist? Or how about being the first woman Catholic priest? I didn't understand how she could come to a conclusion that she should align herself to represent only one denomination. We were attending a Methodist church and were considered members there because of our attendance and participation, but I never thought of myself as being doctrinally Methodist.

Now, I'm not speaking against the Methodist church. The United Methodist Church is where God chose to get me started, and the Methodist Church blessed my socks off. What I'm trying to say here is that it was in the Methodist church where I learned that my search for God and my belief in Jesus made me a Christian, a follower of Christ. However, because of this knowledge they taught me, the only label I wanted associated with my beliefs was *Christian*.

I tried to keep an open mind and let Melainie do what she thought best, but I never consented that she should enroll. She and our pastor took the initiative to get started without my approval. I sat back and watched how this process took place, and I got more and more disturbed as the weeks and months went by.

I could tell it wasn't sitting well with Melainie either, and the whole ordeal drove us to extremes—so much so that I literally punched my fist through a wall in our house at the end of an unsuccessful attempt to reason with her. I never gave her an ultimatum, but the situation was causing such stress on our marriage that I was preparing myself for something that drastic. Besides, it was pretty embarrassing explaining to my seven-year-old son how a big hole got in our wall.

Then came the final straw. I ran into our good friend Julie and mentioned something about Melainie's candidacy for ordination. Trying to sound like an unbiased and supportive husband, I played it cool and didn't express my true feelings about it. Julie looked me right in the eyes, paused for a minute, and then said to me, "Oh, yeah, I can see why you're a Methodist."

I wanted to scream at her, "I'm a what? A Methodist? Where are the gloves? I'm ready to fight!" I didn't want anyone to consider me as anything but a believer in God, a Christian, and to me that meant I was either a member of all denominations or a member of none. And I wanted my wife to share that same understanding. Before I could even approach Melainie to discuss possible alternatives or options, she resigned her candidacy of her own decision.

The tension in our marriage was over, but we were both restless. We both wanted to know more about God.

A series of events lead us to visit Keith and Julie's non-denominational church, Life Christian Center, at a time when a big revival called the Toronto Blessing was sweeping the country. Quickly, almost overnight, Melainie and I were back on the same page again.

The Toronto Blessing was a move or outpouring of God that spread joy and healing through many churches around the world. It made the national news media often and created a lot of controversy, because this was one of those Holy Spirit encounters that was not rational. Both laypeople and pastors were laughing uncontrollably through the services and acting bizarrely. As you will see, this blessing turned out to be just what Melainie and I needed to break through into the true, supernatural power of God.

Chapter 17
1994

I'M NOT ONE OF THOSE PEOPLE WHO WISH THEY COULD to go back and live life over again, but I would like to relive the year 1994. Better than that, you could just freeze time and keep me in that year forever. That was the year I became a different person.

Once I started attending church, it never again felt like an obligation or duty for me. I was going because it felt good. Sure, I was learning and growing, but the main reason I was there was to get that familiar, comforting feeling from God's presence. To be in God's presence I thought you had to be "holy"—you know, quiet and reserved. Our small Methodist church had a very structured service with soothing organ music and a robed choir of angelic voices. To be respectful and proper, it seemed to me that church should be a similar solemn setting. Well, all that changed when I walked through the doors of Life Christian Center.

With the revival going on there, what I saw and heard blew me away. There were thousands of people in every service, and they held two or three services a day—every day, not just Sundays. The services were like a big party, with everyone laughing, shouting, throwing their hands up in the air, and dancing. They were actually celebrating, and to my great surprise, I could feel that warm, oozy presence of God in the midst of all the commotion.

I was hooked. I wasn't sure what was going on, but it sure had a hold on me. And to my pleasant surprise, it had a hold on Melainie, too. It was quite a bit out of our comfort zone, but we didn't want to miss a single service. We were never in a hurry to leave when the services were over, and we couldn't wait to get back for the next one. We both knew God had something to do with this strange stuff. Then it dawned on me. Ever since Melainie's Walk to Emmaus, she had been telling me, "You need to get the joy of the Lord." Joy? Now that was a silly word. "What do you mean *joy*?" I wondered.

As a guy, I thought *joy* was a girlish word for *happy*, and I already considered myself a happy guy. I didn't think I could get any happier, but when I looked at how wild and excited the people were acting in this revival, I began to see a difference between being happy and experiencing true joy. What those people seemed to be getting was way beyond happy. I didn't know what it was, but I sure did want some of it. I began asking God to do that to me. I prayed, "God, that sure looks like it feels good. If this is real, if this is really something you are doing to people, then I don't want to miss out on anything that is of You. I'd like You to do that to me, too."

The revival services were held almost every night of the

week. People were acting so unusually, I would have thought they were all nuts if that oozy feeling hadn't been getting stronger every time I was there. Both Melainie and I were getting so much insight and knowledge from the teachings in these services that we knew we had found a new home church for ourselves.

A few months later, the church was back to services on Sundays and Tuesday nights only, but the revival wasn't over by any means. People were still falling out in the Spirit, crying, laughing, jerking, and even cackling like a chicken. Yes, I said cackling like a chicken. You name it; they did it. They seemed to get such great pleasure out of the experience that they kept pressing in for more, but despite my prayers for it, nothing like that happened to me.

Tuesday night services usually ran late, so Melainie and I took turns staying home with Derek since we didn't want to keep him out late on school nights.

On Tuesday, September 27, 1994, I was tired. I really didn't want to go to church that night, but I went anyway, just to take my turn. During the service, Pastor Rick stopped dead in his tracks, paused, and interrupted his own message by saying, "God is dealing with me about healing." When he said that, I heard a soft, quiet voice come over my shoulder from behind me and say, "You've been healed." I didn't have to turn around to see who said it. It was that same, not man-not woman voice that I had heard before in our house when I thought Melainie was having her morning time with

God. The feeling of God's presence fell on me like a ton of bricks. I knew I had been healed right then and there of the stomach attacks that had been plaguing me for the past thirty-four years, and when it happened, I wasn't having an attack, I wasn't praying for healing, and I didn't feel a thing.

Pastor Rick only spoke for a few minutes, and then he invited everyone to line up so he could lay hands on us for healing. I stood in line, but I knew I was already healed. As he started coming down the line, I prayed that God would confirm my healing by letting me feel that hot oil or electricity that others were claiming to feel during these services.

Pastor Rick was touching people on their heads fast and hard, and they crashed to the floor. When he got to me, he gently laid both of his hands on the sides of my stomach without knowing I had a stomach problem. I didn't feel a thing. He prayed quickly and went on down the line. The only thing going through my mind was that I was not going to drop to the floor just because everyone else did. I can remember praying, "God, I am not going to fall down unless you knock me off my feet, so I will know this is truly of You."

Pastor Rick didn't get very far past me when I got so dizzy and weak, I thought I was going to faint. I couldn't stay up! I had to lie down on the floor to keep from blacking out and falling. Once I was down, that warm, oozy feeling was flowing through my body much more intensely than any other time before. I felt silly lying on the floor. I didn't want others to see me like that. I wanted to go back to my seat, but I couldn't get up. My arms and legs felt like they had heavy weights or sandbags on them. I was amazed! I couldn't get up, roll over, or move a muscle. No matter how hard I tried, I felt like I was glued to the floor.

As soon as I could move, I crawled back to my seat, so weak it was difficult to sit up straight in the pew. Before long, Pastor Rick asked for people to come forward and explain what had just happened to them. I think I was the first one to go up to the pulpit. I took the microphone from him and explained that I had just been healed of a thirty-four year stomach problem. He asked me how I knew that for sure. My reply was: "God said so. There's no doubt about it. I can feel the difference in my body."

I don't think my reply was exactly what Pastor Rick was looking for. He was probably hoping for someone with more concrete evidence or proof to come forward. I have all the proof he or anyone else could need now: fourteen years after that evening (at the time of this writing), I have not had one single stomach attack since that night. I never rolled on the floor in pain again. I have felt absolutely no stomach pain or internal bleeding since that word came over my shoulder. Thank God! He finally did what no doctors could do.

Maybe you're wondering, like I have, why God waited thirty-four years to do it. I still don't know, and I don't care. Perhaps if God would have healed me any sooner, I would not have sought Him so hard or served in the mission field, and I would certainly not be the person I am today. All that matters to me now is that I will never have to suffer with another stomach attack again as long as I live, thanks to the healing power of God.

I knew He could heal. Look at how He healed my ulcers. Even when I was in the midst of torturous physical pain and it was hard to feel the presence of God, I never gave up or quit trusting in Him. I knew God could end the attacks, but I didn't know if He would end them. I believe that He honored my faith that night, and I'm so thankful for all He's done.

To get rid of an illness that had tortured me for thirty-four years was more than enough. I couldn't imagine how God could do anything better for me—but He did!

Just two weeks after I was healed, Pastor Steve Smith was on the pulpit. Now, he was a big man, and a serious, tranquil person. He was the administrator of the church, and I had met with him previously to discuss some financial issues.

When he started to preach, the Holy Spirit fell on him, and he began to very uncharacteristically jump up and down. He had his eyes closed, his fists clenched, and his arms straight down to his sides. He was laughing one minute and crying the next. He wasn't preaching anymore. He just kept yelling, "Woo-hoo," as he bounced up and down like a jack-in-the-box.

When I saw that, I sat back in my seat and had one of my little talks with God again. It went like this, "Now God, I know some of these people have to be faking this stuff. I don't mean to be disrespectful of Pastor Steve, but I know what a good manager he is. I can't help but believe he is just being a good manager of his congregation by thinking that if he acts like that, then other people will feel free to act up, too." I was pretty certain that some of this "slain-in-the-Spirit" stuff was a put-on.

Two nights later, Melainie returned home from her turn at church on Tuesday night, and I got to find out for myself what joy really feels like and what being slain or drunk in the Spirit was. I was lying in bed when she came in at about eleven o'clock at night. Melainie started to fill me in on the service that night and said, "Oh, by the way, Pastor Rick asked us if anyone had a testimony to give, so I got up and told them about God healing your stomach attacks. I hope you don't mind."

When she said that, the room began to spin around and it felt like the temperature shot up a hundred degrees. I started feeling like I was floating sideways, and there was a tingling sensation all over my body. Melainie was waiting for me to answer her, but I couldn't speak. My lips actually rolled backwards and my mouth stretched open wider than I can pull it with my fingers. My cheekbones puffed up like two golf balls. My eyes were squinted so tight I could barely see—and all of this felt so good. It was wonderful!

I began laughing so hard and loud that Melainie was "shushing" me so I wouldn't wake Derek. I kept getting a rush of feeling running all through my body, and I experienced an enlightening high or drunk feeling. I got a revelation about what life means, and I saw a vision of my family in the future.

During this experience, I was unable to control my speech or my body. I was making all kinds of weird noises, like hissing and grunting sounds. I kept blowing out deep sighs of air that seem to release another rush, and then I'd burst out laughing again in deep, hard belly laughs. My feet kept flopping from side to side and jerking around. At times I cried tears because what was happening felt so good. I couldn't control any of this, and I didn't want it to stop. I could see dark purple images that were sort of bird-shaped or like fire flames that would float diagonally from left to right. When I would see them, I got hot flashes. The hot flashes hit my head and face first and then my feet, but not the bottom of my feet. I just felt it on the sides and top of them, as if a steaming hot towel were draped over them. The flashes were so hot that Melainie got a handkerchief out of a drawer and kept wiping the sweat off of me.

This was joy!

Melainie sat in bed with me and witnessed this entire event. I was able to describe a little of it to her as it was happening, but most of it she saw and heard for herself. All she could do during this time was laugh, pray, and she kept saying, "Get him, Lord!" She wanted to get up and turn the lights on so she could see me even better, but I wouldn't let her. I was too embarrassed by all the strange things happening. She kept shouting and laughing over and over, "You should see your face!"

This experience lasted for a whole hour, and when it was over, I felt the sense of God's presence rise up out of my chest. My face went back to normal, and my body was finally still. I calmly said goodnight to Melainie, and fell asleep right away.

When I got up the next morning, everything looked different and I felt different. Everything had a more three-dimensional look, a visual depth that was never there before. I sensed a deep, peaceful feeling inside me that wasn't there before, either. Nothing on Earth seemed to matter anymore. That experience had changed me so much; I will never be the same again.

I even had a physical change from that experience. The first time I spoke that morning, I noticed that my voice sounded different. I asked Melainie what she thought of my voice, but she said it sounded the same to her. Everyone else said it sounded the same to them, too, but it wasn't the same to me. You know how you can hear your own voice in your head when you talk? Well, I had been listening to my own voice for forty-four years, and that morning my voice sounded so different I couldn't believe it was me. It didn't sound distorted or muffled, like when you have a head cold; it just didn't sound at all like myself. It wasn't the same voice that I had been hearing all my life. It took me a long time to get used to it, and it never changed back to how it used to sound.

So what was that experience? It was what I saw happening to others in revival. It was the baptism of the Holy Spirit. It was what I thought people were exaggerating and faking. It didn't seem logical to me that God would do such strange things. From that night on, I knew that warm, oozy feeling in a different, more personal way—as the presence of the Holy Spirit. Now, when I refer to that feeling, I talk about the Source of it with joy.

I learned that God uses strange experiences like that to change you. It's not for the thrill or pleasure of it. Rather, it is to bring you into a deeper relationship and understanding of Him. Why doesn't God just do this to everyone, like He did it to me? It seems to me that if He did something so extreme to everyone, everyone would believe in Him. However, not everyone needs something that extreme to get to the point where God wants them to be. Other people can get to a deeper relationship and understanding of God much easier than I did. God knew what a skeptical, prove-it-to-me guy I was, and He knew He had to do something that extreme to reach me.

My baptism in the Holy Spirit was so fantastic, I was afraid I would never experience anything that incredible again. Well, I'm happy to report to you that was just the beginning. Often, I will get drenched in the Spirit. It is a blessing that comes over me suddenly, with no forewarning. I can't induce it or make it happen, and I never know when it will be a short, faint occurrence or lengthy, intense one.

Sure, it happens sometimes when sitting in a great praise and worship service at church, but to my surprise—and sometimes, my embarrassment—that wonderful, joyful presence washes over me when I'm shopping at Wal-Mart, driving down the road, watching a movie, mowing the lawn, or doing any normal daily activity. The presence of God will come over me, and I'll feel just as drunk as someone who slugged down a case of beer. I still try to quench it when I'm out in public, because I still care about what other people think of me. I don't want to look like I'm nuts when I'm among people who don't believe in this move of the Spirit or get offended by it.

I have to admit that it really confuses me that people

1994

who think it is normal and perfectly acceptable to get drunk on alcohol and laugh or cry uncontrollably, stumble around, or do other weird things often find the baptism of the Holy Spirit offensive or bizarre. I'm an easy-going guy. I'm tolerant of other people's opinions, but this is where I have to disagree with others.

Now, I'm not naïve. I know there are people who exaggerate and act like they are drunk in the Spirit when they really aren't. I always figured there were people who also exaggerated when speaking in tongues, too. In the Christian faith, some believe that when you receive the baptism of the Holy Spirit, you receive the gift of speaking in tongues. When it happened to me during my baptism, I couldn't control it, so it bothered me when I heard people who could turn it on and off whenever they wanted to. These people referred to it as their "prayer language," but I figured they might not be legitimately speaking in tongues from God.

One day I was driving home from running errands and flipping channels on the car radio when I barely caught the tail end of a statement that some pastor was making. I don't know what station I had or who was speaking, but this is a summary of what I heard:

> ...and don't tell me you don't believe in speaking in tongues unless you have tried it for yourself. If you don't think speaking in tongues is a gift of God, then I have a challenge for you. I challenge you to go home, lock yourself in a room for two hours, and try to speak in tongues non-stop the entire

time. Now, if you'll do that for two full hours, I guarantee you will come out of that room convinced that tongues are a direct communication with God.

"OK," I thought, "I'll take that challenge." So home I went. I walked to our bedroom, locked the door, knelt down beside the bed, folded my hands, and stared at the clock until it said exactly 4:00 p.m. Then I closed my eyes and started making up whatever strange words or sounds I could think of. After trying just a few words, I stopped. It was awkward and it felt downright stupid. Frustrated, I said to God, "I'm sorry, but I can't do this. There is no way I can do this for two hours. God, I can't even make up enough words for two minutes. This just isn't for me."

My attempt was such a fiasco that I gave it up and reopened my eyes. I hadn't moved, so I was still positioned directly in front of the clock. I expected it to say it was still 4:00 p.m., but instead, it was 6:00 p.m. Exactly two hours after I began praying—to the minute! I was convinced.

Now when I'm in a situation that's good or bad and I'm at a loss for words or don't know what to do, strange sounds and foreign words just pop out of my mouth. The New Testament of the Bible explains this as being a gift from God. Even if I have no idea what these utterances mean, God does!

Chapter 18
NO MISTAKES

THE BIGGEST CHANGE IN ME AFTER 1994 WAS AN increased burden in my heart for people of other nations. Food and drinking water, both of which we often take for granted here in America, are almost nonexistent in many parts of the world. I knew pain, and I couldn't bear to see other people suffering and living with physical pain when medicines were available in other, more fortunate parts of the world. These conditions created a desire in me to serve God by going to nations where I could help supply those basic needs for survival and thus ease the pain and suffering of others.

I did some local charity work for needy families and went as far as the Cherokee Nation, an Indian reservation in Oklahoma, but even the worst conditions I found in America were often still better than how people live in other nations. Determined to do what I could, I packed up my healing testimonies and I traveled overseas with every volunteer organization that would take me.

I had four prayer warriors who were responsible for my missionary work over a period of nineteen years: my wife, Melainie; and our good friends Jayne, Kathy, and Julie. By "responsible," I mean it was specifically their prayers that got me home safe and healthy every time. With these women earnestly and diligently praying for me, I was never afraid to go anywhere or do anything. It was their intercession that put God's anointing or, as I called it, "a bubble of protection" around me. I can't overemphasize the power of prayer. Without people supporting you in prayer, you are limiting your potential and leaving yourself vulnerable.

Being a volunteer missionary means you pay your own way. Sometimes I was going to two or three nations in the same year, and the costs to do that were significant. The price isn't just made up of travel-related expenses; that's only the small part. The major amount of funds you contribute goes for the materials, supplies, or cash needed to provide aid to the people you're there to help.

Melainie was still working at Southwestern Bell and I was still operating Christian Works, but I realized we were starting to spend more money than we had coming in. I had organizations calling me and asking me to go with them, so I felt like I couldn't say no. I can remember talking to God as I was writing checks for thousands of dollars and saying, "God, I know it isn't very smart to be paying for another mission trip right now, but I know I have to go. You'll just have to help us make ends meet."

Don't give me any credit here. I wish I could say I was a generous person doing a noble thing, but I wasn't. I was very selfish when it came to money. I didn't want to spend money on anything except cars, boats, and beach vacations. I was struggling and beating myself up for spending so much of our income and savings on missions, but I really didn't have a choice; I couldn't live with myself if I didn't.

I controlled all the money in our house, and I kept detailed, precise records. While preparing my income tax return one year, I saw that it was, indeed, a fact that we had spent more money than we earned that year. Still, our cash assets (or net worth) had increased. I shared that discovery with Melainie, but she didn't pay much attention to it.

In the spring of 1995, I contributed substantial amounts to our local church and the Christian Broadcasting Network (CBN), where I assisted their humanitarian and medical outreach teams: Operation Blessing and The Flying Hospital. It was during that time that I noticed an error in our personal checking account. While balancing the checkbook one month, I realized we had about a thousand dollars more than we should have. I couldn't work it out, so I let it ride, figuring I would find the mistake and correct it the next month. However, when I tried to balance the checkbook the next month, we were almost two thousand dollars over what we should have had.

I told Melainie how messed up our account was, and I contacted the bank about it. I assumed the bank was depositing someone else's funds into our account by mistake, but the bank went over the records and insisted there was no mistake. Now, I knew every cent I had coming in each month, and I had the check stubs to prove it. I had only one direct deposit going into that account, my wife's salary from Southwestern Bell. Other than that, no money was deposited unless I deposited it myself.

When Melainie got home from work that night, I took her down to my office and showed her the bank statements. Standing next to each other at my desk, I filled her in on what was happening. As I did, she gave me her usual reply, "Humph." At her response, the Holy Spirit began to fall on me, and I could sense God was doing something like He had done with the money in my wallet when I started Christian Works. Melainie could sense it, too, and we both knew that we needed to quit investigating it and just sit back and let it happen.

Over the next few months, that account continued to increase beyond the receipted deposits until there was almost ten thousand dollars more in that checking account than there should have been. We didn't ask the bank any more questions. We just thanked God.

In the fall of 1997, Melainie and I led a team of volunteers to India for an international event called Praying Through the 10/40 Window. The term refers to the nations in Africa and Asia between ten and forty degrees north of the equator, where the least evangelized countries in the world are. World evangelist Jack Harris was our spiritual authority for the mission. We took Derek and nine volunteers with us. Our purpose was not evangelism, but rather to serve as an intercessory prayer team preparing the way for missionaries to follow after us and permanently establish ministries there.

As a team, we contributed $28,800 in total for this mission to pay all our bills for transportation, rooms, meals, etc., and including the funds we were donating to ministries there. The currency exchange rate from American dollars to Indian currency (rupees) was about forty to one, which meant we had over one million rupees. Huge stacks of rupees, tied in bundles about three inches thick, filled a whole suitcase in our hotel room.

Every night Melainie and I would balance the books for that day and keep the team on track with our budget plan for the trip. One night we thought we made a mistake because we had a whole extra bundle of money. We counted everything an extra time, and it turned out we did have more rupees left over than the day before.

The next night we opened the suitcase, dumped it out on the bed, and there seemed to be even more bundles of money. We figured this might have been because smaller denominations of rupees would account for more bundles of money, but when we totaled up the receipts of what we paid out versus the amount of money on hand, again, we had more money left over than we should have had.

For several nights, the bundles of money stacked on our bed kept getting bigger instead of smaller. Melainie and I knew quite well what was happening, so we reported it to the team. We didn't get much more reaction out of them than a weak "praise God." I don't think they really took us seriously until the mission was over and it was time to go home.

In a closing meeting, we presented the receipts to the team and proved to them that we had spent and donated all of the groups' funds, plus we somehow spent one thousand dollars more than we started with. And we still had $4,200 left over! This time their reaction and "praise God" was a lot more sincere. We divided up the remaining cash and gave each person on the team $350.

The team returned to the States, but Melainie, Derek, and I stayed in India to do some sightseeing since Derek was born there. I brought three thousand dollars of our own personal funds, stashed separately in a money belt, for this extended tour. Plus, we had our three refunds from the group, totaling $1050. I had no other money in that belt, my wallet, pockets, suitcases, or anywhere else.

The three of us traveled extensively to Delhi, Varanasi, and several of the major cities and tourist spots all across India for the next two weeks. I paid all our bills in cash and made donations to a few ministries along the way. On the plane coming home, I pulled out the paid receipts for those two weeks and totaled them up to $3,150, which meant we should have returned with $900. After we arrived home and began unpacking, I took the money belt off and laid it on the bathroom vanity to count it. When I finished counting it, it totaled $4,000. I had returned home with my original three thousand dollars, plus one thousand more than I left home with.

Soon after we returned from India, I had a meeting with Pastor Jack to report the details and accomplishments of our mission. When I finished telling him about how our money kept growing, he cocked his head sideways and said:

"Gee, I wish I had God multiplying the fish like that for me." When he said that, it felt like I got hit by a bolt of lightning. All along I had been reading the stories in the Bible and thinking to myself, "Wouldn't it be great if God would just prove Himself to people today like He did in the Bible? I'd love to see Him multiply fish in front of people today. Then everyone would believe in Him." Pastor Jack's lightning-bolt statement made me realize that God had supernaturally multiplied our money just like He did the fish. The Bible stories really are true and can be trusted!

Chapter 19

MOST PROFOUND

Remember me telling you earlier that once Melainie and I started praying together, evil spirits began an all-out assault on us? Well, all heaven broke loose on us, too! Our catch-up time at night became more of an intense prayer session than a sharing of current events.

Melainie and I were deep in prayer one night, and as we finished praying, I opened my eyes. My vision seemed foggy, like they had some kind of film over them. I rubbed them several times to clear them, but it wouldn't go away. Melainie had opened her eyes, too, and she was sitting up in bed looking out the doorway into our living room. Without looking over at me, she asked, "Does it seem cloudy in here to you?" I didn't answer her right away. I kept blinking my eyes as the light, bluish-green cloud around us got thicker and more obvious.

By the time I could answer her with a yes, a great feeling of peace and comfort came over both of us. With the presence of the Holy Spirit upon us, we just sat there for a while enjoying the great sight and the euphoric feeling that came with it. The cloud looked to be thicker in our living room than it was in our bedroom. Melainie was content to just stay put, but not me. Remember, I'm a "prove it to me" guy. I got up and walked through the doorway onto our balcony. I looked down and saw that our whole house seemed to be filled with the cloud.

As I walked down the stairs, the cloud swirled and drifted around me. When I got down to the living room, I could see the cloud was in every room of our house. I held both of my hands out in front of me, flapped them, and moved them around in circles and patterns. The cloud swished and floated around my hands and between my fingers. I was awed and amazed by the cool feeling of the cloud brushing against my face as I walked around.

My mind went blank. I was too overtaken by the cloud to think about anything except the heavenly feeling of being in it. This was a breathtaking experience.

I walked through the kitchen, opened the back door, and stepped out on to our deck. The air outside was still, and it was a cool, absolutely clear night. The air was clean, crisp, and the moon and stars were shining brightly. I walked out to the edge of the deck and turned around to look back at the house. I could see through the glass storm door and the large picture window next to it. The cloud inside was drifting slightly, turning over in slow motion, and filling every inch of space inside the house.

I walked back in and slowly made my way back to our bedroom. Melainie was either sleeping or enjoying the presence of God with her eyes closed, so I didn't disturb her. I eased back into bed and slowly drifted off to sleep myself, with the most indescribable, peaceful feeling all around me. I woke up a few hours later and looked through the doorway into the living room. The cloud was gone and it was as crystal clear inside the house as it was outside. That great euphoric feeling I had experienced in the midst of the cloud was gone, too.

It took years before I could tell this testimony without choking up. I'm an emotional and sensitive guy, and the thought that God would do something this majestic and supernatural for me was overwhelming. There's nothing I could have ever done in my life that would have qualified me to receive such a spectacular blessing from God.

***

One of the recent trends in the church today are home groups, small groups of people that meet on a regular basis in people's houses to pray, study, and share about their spiritual growth or needs with each other. Our church called these Life Groups, and Melainie and I held one every Friday night in our home.

Those meetings produced sensational results. The highlight was a woman who saw a vision of an angel in our living room. Through that vision, she was healed of cancer!

One night after our meeting was winding down, I ended up in a discussion with two women, Karen and Doris, and somehow the subject of God's cloud of glory came up. This was just weeks after Melainie and I experienced that phenomenon in the very same living room we were sitting in.

I told you I'm no different than you are. Even though I promised not to doubt God again, and even though Melainie had witnessed demons and the cloud with me, my mind started letting doubt creep in. I wanted to tell Karen and Doris what happened to us, but it seemed too preposterous to believe. If I had a hard time believing it, how could I expect others to believe a testimony like that?

Regardless of what they might have thought of me, I took a deep breath and in almost disbelieving manner I began to share the details of what we saw and felt. As I spoke, another cloud started to appear at the top of the ceiling. And this time it wasn't drifting and flowing, but still and heavy looking.

I stopped talking and just watched it drop like a curtain. Both Karen and Doris took a quick gasp of air and closed their eyes. One of them squeaked a little *oh* out loud, and then both of them started to pray softly. I watched as the cloud came halfway down the walls and stopped. It was still way above our heads when it reversed direction and went back upwards and disappeared.

This definitely was not the cloud of glory, because I got the message loud and clear from this ominous sign that God was not pleased with my doubting attitude. I leaned back on the couch and beat myself up again. I had to ask myself, "After all the supernatural stuff that has happened to me, what is it going to take for me to stop doubting my own testimonies?" I had to hang my head down again and apologize to God, and as always, God was listening.

Later that year when I was on a mission trip to Guatemala, one of the women on the team sat down in the seat right in front of me as we were boarding a bus to head home. Before the bus started to move, she swung around and said to me, "I'm sorry, but I need to ask you to forgive me. When this trip started I didn't like you very much. After you gave your testimony about how God filled your house with the cloud of glory, I was jealous of you. I have prayed, and studied, and fasted, and done everything I can do to serve God, and He's never done anything like that for me." All I could say in response to her was, "I know—in God's eyes I'm no better than you. I don't know why He would do that for me, either."

In January 1996 I was in the midst of remodeling my office in our basement. While sanding a two-by-four board, I jammed one of my little fingers into an exposed nail and cut it severely. It was about four o'clock in the afternoon. It didn't bleed very much, so after I bandaged it up I tried to keep working a little longer. I hate to admit it, but I'm a little weak-kneed when it comes to blood and guts, especially my own. In fear that it would resume bleeding, I stopped bending and moving it altogether.

It was Melainie's turn to go to church that night, and I stayed home with Derek. Melainie went straight from work to church, and she didn't get home until bedtime. While getting ready for bed, I told her what I did, unwrapped the finger, and showed it to her. She gasped when she saw it and exclaimed, "Roy, you should have gotten that sewed up!"

I got real huffy with her and snapped back, "God

knows what I've done to my finger. He'll take care of it. We shouldn't have to go running to the doctor for every little thing!" Then I stormed into our bathroom and hung my head down. I didn't have to use the bathroom; I just wanted to get out of Melainie's sight because I felt so bad for talking so harshly to her.

I never apologized to her, but while I was hiding in the bathroom I whined to God, "Gee whiz, God, what in the world is wrong with me? I can't believe I acted like that. I don't know what got into me."

The pain in my finger was so bad, the throbbing kept me awake all night. The next day, Melainie was to stay home from work so we could go to church for a special weekday service with a guest speaker, Evangelist Rodney Howard-Browne, who had inaugurated the Toronto Blessing into our congregation. By the time she woke up, I was unable to bend the finger. It was black and blue, with a wide, gaping cut from the first knuckle all the way down to the tip of my finger. From the looks of it, I had severed some nerves or tendons.

It felt better without a bandage on it, so I left it uncovered. Not long after the ten o'clock service began, Pastor Rodney told everyone to put his or her hands up in the air and praise God. Now, I was still a reserved person, and doing something like raising my arms up in the air was uncomfortable for me. I looked around to make sure no one was looking at me, and I raised both of my arms up over my head.

When I did that, the pain in my finger increased, so I thought to myself, "OK God, I give up. When this service is over today, I guess I'll have to go to the doctor and have him take a look at my finger." As that thought ran through my mind, the pain stopped. With my arms still up in the air, I started praying silently, "Thank You, God, for taking that pain away." When I was done thanking God for giving me some relief from the pain, I lowered my hands and looked at my fingers. I went into total shock. There was no trace of any injury on any one of my fingers, not even a scar or any indication of where the cut was. This was only minutes after walking in the door of our church with that ugly gaping cut!

I stared at my fingers for a little while, and then I nudged Melainie, who was standing right next to me. She opened her eyes, and I held my hands in front of her so she could see all ten of my fingers at once. She looked at my hands, then she looked up at me and asked, "Which finger was it?" She didn't act surprised or say anything else.

We just stared at each other, completely silent, and didn't tell anyone at church about it. We felt like zombies. We went home that day and didn't say a word about my finger to each other for a long time to come. Every time I thought about it, the Holy Spirit would fall on me and render me useless. I would laugh and cry, snort, and giggle until the Spirit lifted and I could think straight again.

We can't remember if it was weeks or months, but it was a long time before Melainie and I began to talk about this miracle with each other. We compared our mental notes to confirm all the details. I tried to write it down on paper, but I couldn't. Every time I tried to write down anything about this testimony, such a heavy presence of the Holy Spirit would fall me that I would go numb. The harder I would try to write about it, the more dazed or lost in the presence of God I would get. This was so profound; there were very few people Melainie and I were able to share this testimony with.

Five years later, on July 23, 2001, Pastor Tony Portel from our church told Melainie he was looking for some testimonies to compile. When Melainie told me what Pastor Tony said, I felt an immediate release and knew that I was finally going to be able to put this miracle down on paper. I ran straight into my office and began typing. I sent Pastor Tony an E-mail describing my finger healing that same afternoon. It was the first time I had no problem recording the testimony.

Don't ask me why God would not allow me to write about this sooner. God only knows. Like I said before, when something this supernatural and miraculous happens to you, you are not in a normal state of mind. You are not even in a normal state of being, so you just can't go around and tell everyone about it like you do when a headache stops after prayer. Something like this leaves you speechless, in awe, and unable to function like normal.

This was the ultimate and most profound miracle Melainie and I have ever experienced. I don't understand why such miracles happen sometimes, when other times it doesn't seem like God is there at all. But whatever happens, it really doesn't matter. I no longer worry about anything, and I no longer doubt anything. Yes, God is real, and that is all that matters!

Chapter 20
GUATEMALA

On one of the mission trips I went on, we held a dental/medical clinic in Guatemala through Operation Blessing. A team of volunteers from El Salvador joined with us for this mission. We set up the clinic in an old, abandoned school complex and provided free treatment and Christian counseling to thousands of people.

My job was to assist an El Salvadoran dentist named Claudia. There were a few difficulties to overcome along the way. First, I have always had a weak stomach. I get sick at the sight of my own blood, and there I was serving as a dental assistant. I could have asked for another assignment, but I was there to do whatever was needed. I was determined to rely on God to give me the ability to endure the bloody mess and be a good assistant. Furthermore, I couldn't speak Spanish, and Claudia couldn't speak English. We didn't have an interpreter, so Claudia and I communicated through our own system of hand signals and words that we made up as we went along.

There were five dentists, but only one spoke enough English that I could converse with him. We lined the dental stations up in a row in a small, one-room building. There were no partitions or privacy between the chairs, so each patient could see and hear what was happening to the other patients.

Thanks to a portable generator, we could do fillings, but mostly we extracted teeth. The scene reminded me of the old *MASH* movie or TV series. We pulled so many teeth, and I wasn't even fazed by the blood and gore. What did faze me was the pain. The Guatemalans were used to pain, but they were not used to needles. They were more afraid of a syringe with a needle on it than pain, so most of our patients refused to take the shots of painkiller. Instead of screaming or grunting when they felt pain, they had a way of shaking their hands that resembled playing a guitar. The more pain they felt, the faster and harder they shook their hands.

I was assisting Claudia one day as a young boy was being treated by another female dentist in the chair next to us. They ran into trouble trying to extract one of this boy's wisdom teeth. They kept offering pain-killer shots to the boy, but he refused. Multiple dentists attempted to pull the tooth, but it wouldn't budge. In the meantime, the boy became increasingly scared, crying and thrashing about in the chair. I kept assisting Claudia with our own patient this whole time, listening to that boy crying and groaning. I looked over at him and he reminded me of my own son, Derek.

The thought of that being my son going through such pain and suffering was more than I could bear. After rolling on the floor in pain with stomach attacks for thirty-four years, I know what its like to suffer with pain. Having had enough, I got desperate to help that boy. I left Claudia's side and went over to him. The only part of him that I could touch without getting in the way of the dentist and assistants were his feet, so I knelt down and grabbed both of them.

I wasn't at a point in my life where I was free enough to pray in tongues in front of other people, so I prayed in English. The boy couldn't have understood a single word I was saying, but he stopped crying, stared down at me, and listened intently as I held his feet and prayed for him.

As I was praying, I could see a physical change come over him. The others could see it, too. It started on his forehead and moved down his body, as though he were experiencing the same the rubber band feeling I sensed moving through my body as I was receiving my healing in Haiti. We were actually watching the Holy Spirit of God flow though him.

Everyone stood still for a minute gazing at the boy as he began smiling and even laughing. With the boy calmed down, the male dentist finished removing his tooth. The boy never twitched or made another sound. In fact, he smiled and laughed as the dentist sewed an incision in his gum back together. When the boy got out of the chair to leave, he staggered around like a drunk, still smiling and laughing as he walked out the door waving good-bye with his mother.

On these medical missions, you have to be very careful what you touch. As you know, the dangers of blood-transmitted diseases are severe. I had to make sure that I didn't have any exposed cuts or scratches, and even with latex gloves on, I made sure none of my cuticles had a crack or split.

I had to wear a mask over my nose and mouth, but I'm not sure if that was to protect me or to protect the patients. I also had to wear goggles. The doctors on this team told me that our eyes are vulnerable to airborne viruses and diseases, so I was never supposed to remove my goggles. In either case, the face mask got me in a little bit of trouble. Since I couldn't speak Spanish and the mask kept them from seeing my mouth to know if I was smiling or frowning, I communicated by shaking my head to say no, and I blinked my eyes to mean "yes" or "that's good." After a few days of what I thought was working as simple communication, one of the Guatemalan interpreters informed me that by blinking my eyes, I was making inappropriate sexual gestures to the women. How embarrassing!

The area of Guatemala we were in was a high plateau in the mountains. It got very hot during the day and very cold at night. After performing my job for a couple days, I was frustrated that my goggles kept fogging up from my own breath. With fogged goggles, I couldn't see well enough to mix the chemicals for the fillings. At one point, I took my goggles off just for a minute to clear them.

While they were off, we had a problem with the operation of the vacuum tubes that drain the mouth while a dentist is working. I checked the system, and found that one of the vacuum bottles that stored all the blood and saliva drainages was too full. My job was to carefully disconnect the bottle and dispose of the contents in a special, biologically safe solution. When I went to unscrew the bottle, the vacuum malfunctioned, or belched, and shot the contents of the bottle right up into my face and into my eyes.

On mission teams like this, you start every morning and close every evening with a group meeting. That night at the closing meeting, Dr. Chris, the team leader, was discussing the extreme importance of safety at the clinic. He explained how extra careful we must be around the blood and saliva and went on and on telling us how serious this situation was. The longer Dr. Chris talked, the harder my heart pounded. He explained, "Breaks in the skin such as cuts, fissures, or abrasions, as well as the mucous membranes of the mouth and eyes are entry points through which blood transmitted disease can infect us. These diseases can be absorbed right through the mucous membranes of your eyes." When Dr. Chris said that, I thought my heart was going to pop out of my chest. I politely interrupted him and told him about the vacuum collection bottle exploding in my eyes earlier that day.

There was silence for a minute, and then he replied, "Well, since you washed your eyes out really well, I wouldn't be too worried. But let's pray for you." He gathered the whole team around to lay hands on me and pray. As the team started rebuking the germs and diseases that I was exposed to, the Holy Spirit fell on me and I began laughing and smiling, just like the young Guatemalan boy had done when I prayed for him.

Whatever that unnatural joy in the Spirit is, it is definitely comforting and an assuring feeling of God's presence. When I walked off to go to bed that night, I was dizzy, light-headed, and felt like I was drunk. During the night,

I woke up, still feeling drunk. It felt like someone put a patch over my left eye and a tight bandage around my head. I woke myself up over and over again that night trying to pull the patch off or loosen the bandage, but every time I did that I found there was nothing there. I thought I was just dreaming.

The patch and bandage felt so real, I actually got up out of bed one time and looked in a mirror to see if I could see anything. The mirror confirmed that there was nothing there, but every time I got back to sleep, the same feeling would wake me up again. This kept going on all night long. By morning that strange sensation had finally gone away.

Near the end of the trip, Dr. Chris came up to me and asked me how I was feeling. He acted happy but surprised when I told him I felt great, as if he had expected me to be sick or something. He asked about my eyes and vision, and I told him they were fine. Since I had his personal attention, I shared with him about the sensation I had of the patch over my eye and the tight bandage around my head. Dr. Chris looked at me with an astonished look on his face. He smiled and said, "Roy, we didn't want to alarm you and get you overexcited, but what happened to you was serious. We were so concerned for your health that we continued praying for you after you went to bed."

At the writing of this testimony, it has been thirteen years since that bloody mucus got into my eyes and I have never experienced any illnesses or diseases from it. I've recently had blood work done for a checkup and the results showed that I'm in perfect health.

Near the end of that Guatemala mission, I had seen enough blood and gore. I was starting to have nightmares of pulling teeth. I told Nancy, the nurse in charge of scheduling our assignments, and she recommended that I take a day off and assist Dr. Brown with some appointments he had in the community.

The first stop on our agenda was to visit the local hospital. After introductions, we were escorted around to view the facility, which was a rundown concrete block structure with a clay tile roof. Patient recovery rooms were small, eight-foot-square cubicles with an elevated concrete slab for a bed in the middle of the room.

There was a ventilation block in each room that let light and air in, but no window. To recuperate, the patients laid on the concrete slabs with a pillow and blanket.

The last thing they showed us was one of their operating rooms. They failed to tell me there was an operation in progress, and I never assumed there would be one, even when they had me put on a gown, mask, and shoe covers; I thought they just wanted to keep the room sanitary.

Well, as we walked up to the operating room, the first thing I noticed were the swinging doors. They didn't close all the way, and I could see flies passing through the gap between them. When the doors swung open, a man having leg surgery was laying on an operating table so close I could have touched him. This sight wasn't quite the relief I needed from working with the dental patients.

No one said a word as I looked each one of the nurses and the doctor in the eyes. They all looked into my eyes, and then the whole room started to go dark. The pungent odor in the room overpowered me. They could tell I was about to faint, so Dr. Brown quickly escorted me out of the room, sat me down in a chair, pushed my head down between my knees, and handed me a cup of coffee. I told Dr. Brown I didn't drink coffee, and he said, "You'll drink this one." He was right. I drank every drop and never even tasted it.

Once I had recovered, I asked about the prognosis of the man with the broken leg and was told that there was not much hope for him. The doctors explained that many people in Guatemala who are injured die from infections, whether they receive medical attention or not, due to the lack of sanitary conditions in people's homes and the difficulty in obtaining simple first-aid supplies to maintain care.

Remember me telling you that my prayer warriors were responsible for me getting home safe and healthy from these mission trips? Julie prayed for me without any specifics, just as a matter of her daily prayer routine. But before I would leave home, I would give Melainie, Jayne, and Kathy a complete itinerary and agenda of my trip. The agendas would be so detailed that the girls would know exactly where I was and what I was doing at every hour of the day. I even converted the hours on the agendas from the time zone of the country I was in to the time at home so they would be praying for the correct thing at the time it was actually happening.

Because of the remote places I would travel to, I never communicated with home until I arrived back in the United States. Phone lines in underdeveloped countries were hard to find and, if one could be located, it was often even harder to get a connection. It was rare to actually be able to hear who you were trying to talk to. However, after I returned home, we would compare notes, and many times the notes would show that without any communication between us, my intercessors sensed needs or dangers at the same time I was having a need or problem.

The sincerity and devotion of their prayers were so powerful I often thought I could actually feel them. At times, the prayers of these three women literally had the power of life over death—my life! Their prayers influenced the effects of the natural and supernatural powers I was experiencing in the field.

Chapter 21
JUST DO IT

I WAS IN COSTA RICA ONE TIME WITH A JOINT Methodist-Catholic building project. Our team of about twelve men and women constructed an entire second-story addition to a church school building. There is such a great feeling of personal satisfaction when you do something of this magnitude for someone else, that no thanks from anyone is even remotely necessary. But the people you are serving are so grateful they find it hard to do or say enough to show you their appreciation.

In this community they held a celebration in our honor at the home of one of their most prominent congregation members. We were informed by the local pastor that the family hosting us for this celebration had sacrificed much in order to present our team with a gift worthy of their most sincere thanks.

The home was small, but it was considered a grand household because they had electricity, as evidenced by a one low-watt bulb dangling on a wire from the ceiling. It would have made sense (and taken less space) if we could have all remained standing, but that was not an appropriate way to honor someone in their culture. So we were all seated in a circle in a room so small we literally sat on each other's legs and laps, with all of our knees overlapping in the center. After a prayer and words of thanksgiving, a foreword was given as to the great sacrifice this family made to be able to provide us with the special gift of a refreshment. Upon that remark a silver tray was delicately passed in through the doorway of the home, and on the tray was one small bottle of Coca Cola. We sat there in silence choking on our tears, as they proudly served each one of us their monumental treat, a tiny shot-glass full of soda that wouldn't mean a thing to anyone back home.

Whatever type of mission trip I went on, my underlying goal was to help ease the physical pain and suffering of others. I only went on one mission that was pure evangelism. Pastor Jack Harris held a crusade in 1995 called Fire in Costa Rica, referring to the fire of God. Pastor Jack took us into the banana plantations of Costa Rica for a Holy Ghost revival.

I was one of nine assistants Pastor Jack took along for prayer support, to counsel new believers, and to be a witness of God's salvation and supernatural powers. From time to time, Pastor Jack would call one of us up to the pulpit to give a testimony of what God has done in our lives. Now, I could handle that. I don't like to speak in front of large groups, but I am willing to do anything that gives me a chance to tell one of my testimonies and thank God for it.

At one of the night meetings in a recreation field, a crowd of at least two thousand people gathered to hear Pastor Jack. That evening he was speaking about healing. At one point, the crowd was so stirred up and reacting so emotionally to Pastor Jack's message, I just knew he was going to call on me to give my testimony. When he didn't, I was crushed.

I thought the whole purpose in my being on that team was to tell others about my documented healing from stomach ulcers. I thought Pastor Jack really missed the timing on that one; I thought he should have called me up when the people were so engrossed in what he was saying. Near the end of his message that night, Pastor Jack finally did call on me to share my testimony. As I walked up the stairs onto the handmade stage, I can remember thinking to myself: "Sure, Jack, now you call on me after people are starting to leave and not paying as much attention. How is this going to help get anybody healed? It's too late now."

I took the microphone and gave the Spanish interpreter a nod to introduce me. Speaking through an interpreter was disorienting. It's difficult to maintain your chain of thought and project your emotions through the delayed reaction of an interpreter. Nevertheless, once I started giving my testimony of my healing in Haiti, that wonderful Holy Spirit showed up and all my criticism and concerns fell away. Looking out at the faces in the crowd, I realized that it didn't matter if everyone was paying attention to me or not. If just one person heard what I was saying, then I knew it would be worth it.

Pastor Jack closed the meeting by asking everyone who needed healing to come forward and let our team lay hands on them and pray. That was something else I was not comfortable with. It was different when God lead me to pray for that boy in Guatemala. I knew I was supposed to do that; I could sense the Holy Spirit guiding me. But to be instructed to go lay hands on people? I didn't have any special anointing or gift of God to do that, but I was there to serve Pastor Jack. I decided that if that was what he wanted me to do, I certainly would do my best.

Several hundred people came forward. I walked through the crowd laying hands on anybody who wanted me to pray for them. This went on for quite a while. I wasn't feeling especially godly or spiritual while I was doing this. In fact, I wasn't feeling anything but uncomfortable. I thought, "If God were healing somebody through my prayers, wouldn't I know it or feel it?" I didn't think I was really helping anyone, but I kept praying for them anyway.

As I walked around, I kept passing by the same man lying on the ground. I noticed several other team members had already prayed for him, but he was still in the same place. There were two other Costa Rican men standing beside him the whole time. I finally stopped walking past them and asked what was wrong with the man on the ground. The man was holding his sides, moaning and groaning. He couldn't speak English, but one of the other men could.

They proceeded to tell me that earlier that day the man on the ground had been in a bad car accident. He hurt his stomach and his chest. These two friends took him to a doctor, and after a thorough examination, the doctor informed them he had broken several ribs. The doctor didn't have any pain medication to give the injured man, so all he did was wrap a thick gauze bandage around the man's chest and sent him away. The friends loaded the injured man into the back of a small pickup truck and brought him straight from the doctor's office to the crusade. The friends had to carry the man because he was too badly injured and in too much pain to walk.

With that information, I took my turn. I leaned over and laid my right hand on his head and prayed for his healing. Nothing. They didn't even thank me when I finished. The man was still moaning and groaning as I walked away.

There were plenty of others to pray for, but I kept looking back at that same man on the ground. It was getting late, and the crowd was getting a little thinner. Still, that man was lying motionless and crying out in pain. His pain got to me. I couldn't stand it anymore. I began to plead with God to help this man, but became increasingly frustrated when nothing happened. The man went on begging for help as his friends stood helplessly at his side.

When his friends decided it was time to leave, they tried to help the injured man get up. As they got him to his knees, he bellowed out in pain, and when he did, the fire in Costa Rica fell on me. I got a hot flash that felt like somebody poured hot oil all over me. I rushed over to the man and knelt down on the ground with him.

I was angry. I mean, really angry! I was so angry at whatever accident, spirit, or reason there was for this man being in so much pain that I'm sure I startled everyone around us with my harsh, mean attitude. I grabbed the man and roughly shoved my left hand down through the neck of his shirt and placed it over the bandage on his chest.

I closed my eyes, threw my right hand straight up in the air and shouted out, "God, I can't bear to see this man in such pain. Lord, take this pain away from him. Give it to me, God. Let me have his pain; just don't let him suffer anymore." As I was praying those words, my hand felt kind of hot, but I figured that was just the man's body heat. Then the man suddenly became silent.

I opened my eyes and he was looking right back at me with his mouth hanging open. He looked at his friends and started speaking to them in Spanish with a wide-eyed look on his face. The English-speaking friend got really excited and told me, "My friend says that the pain has stopped. He has no pain whatsoever. It all went away."

The injured man slowly got up to his feet without help and began to move around. He started twisting and bending, and there was no pain. We took the man to Pastor Jack and told him what had just happened. Pastor Jack handed the man a microphone and the man began telling everyone over the loudspeaker system how God had just healed him.

I never got to talk to that man again. The last sight I had of him, he was up on that stage by Pastor Jack with his hands high in the air, jumping up and down shouting praises to God.

Chapter 22
A GOD THING

BOLIVIA, MEXICO, AND Brazil WERE A FEW MORE OF the nations I served on medical mission teams for Operation Blessing and The Flying Hospital. On the Operation Blessing missions, small teams traveled to remote villages in jungles and rain forests treating people who had never seen a doctor or dentist before. The Flying Hospital missions were large scale, with over a hundred doctors and assistants on each team. The Flying Hospital was just what it sounds like: a huge L-1011 jet had been gutted and all the seats were replaced with operating and recovery rooms. The plane took us to countries to perform free medical treatments and surgeries to masses of impoverished people.

In 1998 I went to Bolivia with The Flying Hospital and helped give eye examinations so that people could be fit with reading glasses. We were in Cochabamba, which is one of the highest airport elevations in the world. The altitude was 9,000 feet, which caused several of our team members (including me) to get minor nosebleeds just by bending over to tie our shoes.

Among the people there was a tribe of descendants from an ancient indigenous sect who had their own unique, tribal language. My job was to lead the patients through an eye chart to help determine what strength of glasses they would need. This was a painfully slow process. Every letter on the chart had to be communicated through three interpreters starting with me saying the phrase "Read the first letter" to a Spanish interpreter who repeated it to a Portuguese interpreter. The Portuguese interpreter then translated the phrase into the tribal language for the patient. Every answer had to come back up the chain of interpreters—all three of them—the same way. After only a few days of this, I was actually happy when a patient couldn't read past the first letter.

///

In January 2000, I went with The Flying Hospital to Puebla, Mexico, at the base of a gigantic active volcano. It was a little unnerving driving around that volcano every day, watching the clouds of smoke constantly trailing away in the wind and knowing an eruption could occur at any time.

The plane was used for cataract operations and other simple surgeries at an outlying airstrip. Besides that, three local hospitals assisted us with minor orthopedic surgeries, and we set up a large clinic in an old warehouse for general examinations.

Only a few hundred patients were treated at the plane

and hospitals; the bulk of the patients went through our warehouse clinic. In total, we treated 8,712 patients in only ten days. Some of those patients walked for seven days to just get to our clinic, and many of them waited and slept in line another four days to get to see a doctor.

What was my job this time? I went along as the go-to guy, to be a pair of hands to do whatever grunt work was needed. I helped register patients, performed crowd control out on the streets, kept the doctors stocked with supplies, and helped coordinate and distribute meals to the team.

After the first week in Puebla, the manager of the clinic was called home due to a family emergency. Someone was needed to fill his shoes and coordinate the entire clinic for the remainder of the mission. Guess who got elected? Me.

The CBN staff on this team was aware of my previous experience with their missions, so they approached me in confidence to get my reaction to the possibility of managing the whole clinic—all 125 doctors, 135 interpreters, eighty support assistants (including me), and ten security guards. The last thing they said to me was, "So, how about it? Are you willing to step up to the plate?"

I not only stepped up to the plate, I picked up the bat and hit a home run. Please don't think I'm bragging. I'm not patting myself on the back for this. Once I said I'd give it a try, the Holy Spirit took control of things, and I got to stand there and watch it happen. I could never have managed that clinic in the natural. It had to be a God thing.

Here's one example of what my days were like: At one point, Dr. Bill came rushing to me in a panic from our eye examination station. He explained that he was running out of the most common lens prescribed. Dr. Bill was in a tizzy, exclaiming that we needed to find more lenses and find them right away. I took his "we" as meaning "me" and started trying to figure out what to do. I had no authority to purchase anything, and even if I had, I wouldn't know where to start looking. The probability of finding any eyeglasses at all was practically zero. They weren't available in this area of Mexico, which is precisely why we were there.

This was a matter I would have to present to The Flying Hospital Staff. I never even got a chance to write the need down on my to do list because of the constant stream of team members coming to me with questions and asking for instructions. However, later that day, a team member was casually walking past me when, for no apparent reason, he stopped and said to me, "Hey, I don't know if this will do you any good or not, but when my interpreter took me souvenir shopping last night we ran across a little shop that either makes eyeglasses or stores them. They had all kinds in stock there if we need anything." As it turned out, they had exactly the type of lens we were running out of.

That was how the rest of that clinic was managed. I didn't have to seek solutions to anything. God met every need by sending the right person at the right time, right to me.

Out of the thousands of patients we treated in that clinic, the one that amazed me the most was an unconscious gentleman that was brought in on a stretcher.

I escorted the stretcher to the next doctor available and

helped lift the man from the stretcher onto an examination table. When we held the man in our hands to move him, he moaned in a strange-sounding voice, but he didn't wake up. As soon as we set him down, he was silent and still. No one knew where this man came from or what was wrong with him. I left the patient with an American doctor and returned to my post at the clinic entrance. The doctor tried to wake the patient for examination, but every time the doctor touched him, he moaned and groaned and tried to pull away.

A Spanish interpreter assisted the doctor by holding the patient, and the patient never made a sound. They tried it again. When the doctor touched the patient, he groaned and withdrew, but when the interpreter touched the patient, he stayed still and quiet. The man never opened an eye once to see who was touching him.

We sent in a second doctor from our American team, and the patient groaned and pulled away from that doctor, too. Then we sent in a third doctor, a local. The Mexican doctor had no problem touching and examining the patient at all. The patient laid still and quiet the whole time, but the Mexican doctor could find no reason for the man to be unconscious; there was nothing apparently wrong with him. The news of what was happening with this patient spread around the whole clinic.

When I heard what was going on, I left my post and went back to see for myself. When I got to the room the man was in, no one else was there. The man was lying facing the wall, so I reached out and lightly touched his upper left arm. When my fingers touched him, he didn't move, but he made a deep, growling sound. I tried it a second time, and the same thing happened. A couple of doctors walked in while I was still standing there and said, "Roy, do you know what's going on here?" Before I had a chance to say anything, they continued, "This guy isn't sick, he's demon-possessed. We finally figured out that he only groans and pulls away when a Christian touches him. If it's not a Christian, it has no effect on him. We're going to pray for deliverance."

I went back to my post as a group of doctors, pastors, and spiritual counselors from our team and the local area went to work over that man praying and rebuking demons. I don't know how long it took, but they reported to me later that day that they prayed until the man regained consciousness.

When he woke up, he was a friendly man, but he had no idea where he was or what had happened to him. The doctors examined him thoroughly, but found nothing else wrong with him. I don't know what happened to that man after he left the clinic, but I'll bet you he's a Christian today.

※

The last day of the clinic, I had to go out into the streets and tell hundreds of people who were still waiting in line that our time was up, we had to leave, and that those still waiting in line would not get to see a doctor. To make the announcement, I grabbed a portable loudspeaker and climbed on top of a fifty-gallon metal barrel so everyone could see and hear me better. When I finished the announcement, the crowd mobbed me!

They grabbed me and lifted me down off the barrel. I was caught so much by surprise; I had no idea what they were going to do to me. Once they had me down off the barrel, they began hugging and kissing me. They gave me gifts, sang a love song to me, and thanked me just for coming to them, even though they never got to see a doctor. Oh, how that melted my heart.

Chapter 23
RAISE YOUR HANDS

THE SCOPE OF THE FLYING HOSPITAL WAS QUITE an extreme contrast to the small Operation Blessing teams where we were doing really well if we treated eight hundred people in a two-week period. I went to Brazil twice with these small, twelve-member teams. Both times we packed our little medical clinic into old, wooden boats and traveled to remote jungle villages along the Amazon River.

We started out from the city of Manaus, where the Rio Negro and Amazon River merge. The Rio Negro was filled with coal black water. I don't mean dirty. I mean it was actually coal black in color. The extreme amount of decay from the jungles that runs off into the water is what gives it that color. If you stick your hand just barely an inch under water, your skin looks a deep orange color. If you stick it down deeper than an inch, you can't see your hand at all.

The Rio Negro water won't even mix with the muddy brown Amazon water. Alongside one another, they look like a blacktop road sitting next to a dirt road. As a boat moves through them, the propellers stir the waters together, but as the boat passes, you can watch as the waters separate back out to brown and black, with a definite division line between them.

Before we left Manaus, our team toured a Center for Tropical Diseases, where a lot of research was done formulating antidotes and treatments for infections. It was fascinating seeing all the snakes, spiders, and other creepy-crawly things. The most fascinating part was hearing some of the facts they gave us. They told us that they currently had a list of over 1,100 tropical infections that they didn't even have names for yet.

I was only allowed to take what I could fit in two tiny duffel bags, each two feet long and one foot wide and deep. The humidity in the Amazon was so high that I took off wet clothes every night and put wet clothes on every morning. We lived right on the boat, which was furnished similar to a traveling motor home, only much smaller. My personal cabin was three feet wide, five feet long, and the ceiling was so low I couldn't stand up straight. With my bed being less than five feet long and my height standing at nearly six feet, I had to keep my knees bent the whole time I was in bed. Can you imagine sleeping like that for two weeks?

A Brazilian captain and a cook came along with the boat, which resembled a tiny steamboat without the paddle wheel. We ate a lot of water buffalo meat that was dried out in the sun on top of the boat, a baby alligator, and even some piranha. The boat had a huge electric generator on board that ran about twelve hours a day. It was deafeningly loud—literally. It probably contributed to the slight loss of hearing in my right ear today, since it was the ear that was always facing the generator.

The boat would take us up the river to small villages where we would operate our small clinic of doctors, dentists, nurses, a pharmacist, and of course, a spiritual counselor. The specific villages we were to visit were prearranged since we could only visit villages that had a small, empty building or shelter near the waters edge that we could use for the clinic. At each village, we would haul all our gear ashore across the narrow gangplank and set up our makeshift examination rooms. Then a day or two later, we would tear down our clinic and haul everything back across the gangplank. You had to have good balance carrying the cargo. It was often like walking a tightrope.

Some dental work was done on these trips, but it was limited almost exclusively to tooth extractions because we seldom used a portable generator for electricity. There certainly were no surgeries performed. The primary treatment we provided under these conditions was distributing medications.

Most of the patients were local to whichever village we were in, but many would arrive by river in a hollowed-out log canoe, all dressed in their best attire. I never could figure out how they could get their white clothes so immaculate and brilliantly clean by washing them in such muddy brown water.

Usually the villages were centered around one building, with most of the homes widely spread out. Those houses were either on stilts to avoid flooding or built like rafts anchored by ropes to trees so they could float up and down with the river level. In either case, they looked like elaborate tree houses due to the raw wood construction and tin roofs. In spite of their lack of electricity, nearly every home had a TV antenna on the roof. The people used car batteries to power the television sets. Often, we would see a canoe pass us with a couple car batteries on board heading to a generator somewhere for a charge.

One house I saw really bothered me. It was floating so low that the door opening was actually level with the water. As we passed, I saw a huge alligator floating in the water with his snout pressed right up to the opening. There was nothing keeping that gator from walking right in. I would have never been able to sleep in that home!

Wherever we went, the people were always warm, friendly, and so grateful. You didn't have to speak their language to feel their love. The villages usually had a chief or elder who was the spokesman and leader for their community.

At one of the villages, a blind woman was hand-led by her relatives into the clinic for help. The doctors examined her closely, and the diagnosis was bad: she had severe and complete cataracts. There was nothing our doctors could do for her but pray, so pray they did! That woman didn't walk out of our clinic without holding on to a guide, but she did receive some of her sight back. After the prayers, she was able to see shapes and count fingers, neither of which she could do before the prayers.

There are no roads in the Amazon jungles. The only way in and out is by boat. We were scheduled to stop our boat and hold a clinic at a different village almost every day.

For some reason, it was determined suddenly one day that we were to skip one certain village and not set up there. Days later, a messenger from that village caught up with our boat and informed us that the night we were supposed to arrive there, the whole village was engulfed in what they call a cloud of mosquitoes. When this happens, the mosquitoes are so dense no one can breathe. The whole village had to be evacuated. We thanked God for sparing us from that calamity and informed the messenger that we would visit their village on our way back.

We continued up river and arrived at the next village very early in the morning. Everyone in this village was upset and mourning because just a few nights before we arrived, their village chief was swallowed alive by a large anaconda as the chief was sleeping on the ground.

As for me, I slept with a small flashlight in my hand every night. If a bug landed on me in the dark, I had to turn my light on and look at it before I swatted it. There was a certain bug that we were told to carefully brush away, because if the bug were to get smashed on our skin, its urine would cause a severe, flesh-decaying burn.

Despite what you might be thinking, this kind of bold, adventurous life was not for me. I don't even like spiders. At home, I don't even sit outside on my deck because of mosquitoes, and there I was in a jungle with snakes, gators, jaguars, and killer bugs. It was only by the empowering of God that I was able to do such things.

I don't want to sound "holier than thou," like I had some great gift to do this, because I sure didn't. What I'm trying to say is that this was a calling for me. I knew I was supposed to go. I knew it so strongly that nothing could have stopped me from going. I didn't have any specific skills or abilities. All I had was the desire and willingness to help others, and once I said yes to that call, nothing bothered or worried me, wherever He led me to serve.

Remember that bubble of protection I said I always felt? In all of my missionary travels—to thirteen nations in nineteen years—I only got sick one time, and that was an extremely minor illness. I was in leper colonies, malaria-infested areas, villages with the Ebola virus, had infected blood splashed in my eyes, hugged and traded sweat with people dying of AIDS, and I was never affected by anything. The reason for my good health wasn't all the immunizations and preventative medications that I took, although they sure helped. It was my prayer warriors and God's intervention.

That one minor illness that I mentioned happened at a time when almost everyone on the boat got nausea and diarrhea at the same time. We thought maybe the piranha we ate the night before could have caused this illness, but not everyone who ate the piranha got sick. By sheer accident, we discovered the cause. One of the team members was speaking to our cook and saw firsthand what the problem was. The cook had a platform on the back of the boat that she could lower into the water and use to wash our dishes and silverware—in the Amazon River!

We had to bathe ourselves with the Amazon water on these trips, and when we did, we had to be very careful not to get the water in our eyes or on our lips. We knew not to drink anything but the bottled water we brought with us, and the cook knew she was supposed to cook all our food with bottled water. However, no one thought to tell her to wash the dishes and cooking utensils in bottled water, too.

The Brazilian government allowed us to visit one village whose culture and customs they were trying to protect from the influences of external sources, in other words, from the influences of people like us. We were sternly instructed not to give anything to the people there or to leave anything behind. I was told the officials wouldn't even allow *National Geographic* magazine to come into this village and take photographs. We were honored.

With such a build-up as this, I was expecting to experience akin to what I had read about the caveman days. Well, that image was shattered at the first site of the people in that community. They were all wearing T-shirts with name-brand logos on the front. For such a protected environment, we couldn't imagine where they were getting all the modern, factory-made clothes.

We provided medical attention to everyone in the village and were very careful about how we did it. One of our team members was an old Three Stooges fan, so to distract the children while the dentists were working on their teeth, he would raise a smile out of them by making the notorious Curly sound, "Whoop, whoop, whoop," and patting the top of his head.

When it was time to leave their village, our team stood on the side of the boat to say farewell, and the whole community came out to the bank of the river to see us off. As we waved good-bye, every child in the whole village started yelling "Whoop, whoop, whoop" and patting the top of their heads. So much for not influencing the culture!

※

After about a week traveling along the Amazon River, we turned the boat around and started heading home. Like we promised, we stopped at the village that had experienced the mosquito infestation to spend the night. By this time, the cloud of mosquitoes had moved on to another location and our team was welcomed with a great celebration.

They assembled most of the people in that village into a large wooden-slat building with a tin roof. I'm not sure if the building itself was a church, but the village did have a resident Christian pastor. Those that couldn't fit inside the building with us filled the doorways and windows, sitting on top of each other's shoulders to see in. They provided us with a very nice worship service, that is, until I got a bee in my bonnet.

At one point in the service, the pastor asked one of our team members to come forward and give us a word from God. The woman they chose to do this caught me by surprise. I didn't get the impression from her reserved, quiet demeanor that she had the moxie in her to preach to others. Boy, was I wrong.

Not only did she teach and preach, but she did so

extremely well. When she was finished speaking, the village pastor told everyone to close their eyes, raise their hands, and praise God. That's when the hair on the back of my neck stood up again. Just like when my finger was healed, here was another pastor telling me to raise my hands—and even after receiving a healing with my hands in the air, I still wasn't comfortable doing that in front of others. You would think by then I would have had enough experience with spiritual traditions to be more tolerant, wouldn't you? Well, I didn't. I was still holding on to my skepticism of uniformity. To me, God was so concerned with us as individuals that traditional actions in unison seemed impersonal and less meaningful.

I closed my eyes, kept my arms straight down at my sides, and I had another one of my little discussions with God. It went like this, "God, I don't feel like raising my hands just because this pastor said to do it. After all, I don't sense you or the Holy Spirit nudging me to raise my hands, so I'm not going to raise my hands just because some pastor said so." When I got done expressing my reasons for being disobedient, I opened my eyes and looked around the room. Had I ever blown it that time! When I opened my eyes, the room was quiet, and from right above our heads all the way up to the tin roof was the cloud of glory.

It was the very same cloud that filled my house. There's no mistaking it for smoke or anything else. It was that same wonderful light bluish-green color, and it rolled and moved in slow motion, exactly like Melainie and I had seen it do in our home.

This time there was a level, flat bottom to the cloud. The people sitting on each other's shoulders had their heads completely in the cloud. Then I began to notice faces. Everyone who raised their hands like the pastor said to was touching the cloud, and everyone who was touching the cloud was smiling or laughing softly with the most pleasant, peaceful looks on their faces. Everyone who had their arms down at their sides (like me) was solemn, sad, or even frowning. They were looking around the room restlessly, impatiently, like they wanted this subtle, quiet time to be over. Not only was I not feeling that indescribable, great, euphoric feeling that I had when I walked around in the cloud at home, but I was upset and miserable.

I never did raise my hands that night. I was too ashamed of my thoughts, stubbornness, and the way I put my foot down to God. I just kept staring at the cloud. I can't remember when it disappeared or what I did the rest of the night, because I was in great anguish for making such a terrible blunder. It's a shame I had to learn this lesson the hard way.

The good news is that now I raise my hands to God at all opportunities, without someone telling me to do it. The bad news is that God has never allowed me to see His cloud of glory again since that night.

Chapter 24
DO IT YOURSELF

ALL THE MISSIONARY EXPERIENCE I HAD CULMInated in 1999. By this time I felt I had enough confidence and experience to step out and really get my feet wet, so Melainie and I founded our own mission/ministry in Uganda, East Africa.

Uganda is a tiny nation that has endured horrendous persecution and the slaughter of ethnic and religious groups for centuries. Viruses and diseases are widespread, with health facilities and medications scarce to none. Eighty percent of the people live in mud huts with thatched roofs, sleep on straw mats on a dirt floor, and have no electricity and no plumbing. There are several tribal kingdoms with warriors who still walk naked and carry spears. And there are several bands of renegades that roam the country mutilating everyone in their path with machetes. Have you got the picture?

So how in the world did I end up in Masindi, Uganda? I'm no brave, courageous soul. I'm the biggest chicken there ever was. But when God puts it on your heart to do something, you don't have a choice.

Masindi is where I helped build houses for Habitat for Humanity. It is the place where I paced up and down the red clay road and told God I could not go home until He made some sense out of things for me. Ever since my first trip to Masindi, I kept praying, "God, You have got to send somebody to help these people." God kept answering me with this question, who knows those people and what their needs are?

My response was sheer fear: "Oh no, God; not me. I don't want to go back there!" For a whole year I ran scared. I kept telling God my reasons for not wanting to go back—the Ebola virus, which can kill you in hours, not just days; the fact that 18 percent of the people there have AIDS—but I knew I was just wasting time. I didn't have a choice.

Uganda was a British Colony until just fifty years ago, so many of the people there are bilingual. Even in some remote villages you can find people who speak both Swahili and English.

I started receiving letters from a few of the people I met there. Postal service from Uganda was antiquated. It took anywhere from two to eight weeks to get a letter from Masindi to the United States, and to mail a reply back took just as long—if it ever got there at all.

The letters that touched me the most were from children. One eleven-year-old boy wrote this:

Dear Roy,
   I would like to thank God who made my older brother to survive in Kichwamba. It was one morning when they were still sleeping and then came rebels with guns and killed all the children in the school and some were taken to become rebels like them.

Another thirteen-year-old boy wrote to me in agony several times, begging me to come back and rescue him. One of his letters read:

When will you come and collect me? I want to join your family. We shall just escape. I wrote this letter crying.

These kids never knew when some band of rebels would just sweep through their village, steal all they wanted, and slaughter anyone in their path. They had to live with this fear daily. How could I write back and tell those kids I was afraid to return?

For a whole year I stalled, hoping God would release me from the call. I didn't share my thoughts about it with Melainie or anyone else, but I was getting more burdened with it every day. I couldn't live with myself until I went back and tried to do something to make their life better.

Whenever I'm looking for direction or confirmation of what I'm supposed to do, I always look for witnesses. I want to make sure I'm listening to God and not just listening to my own mind. I had been fighting with my mind over this compelling need to go back to Africa. I needed a definite witness that this was really God's plan and not my own.

I wasn't quite ready yet, but I knew it was time I broke the news to Melainie about what I was thinking. We were sitting in a pew one night after a three-day fast for our church. Melainie and I left a little space between us so we wouldn't distract each other while praying in silence. We were supposed to be praying for our church, but the only thing on my mind was how I was going to tell Melainie I had to go back to Masindi.

"OK God, here I go," I prayed. "Please give me the right words to say to Melainie so she will understand what I have to do." I opened my eyes and looked over at her. At the very same time she turned to look at me with tears running down her face. Before I could say a word, Melainie said, "You have to go back to Africa, don't you?" I didn't need any stronger witness than that.

※

Melainie and I decided that we would do a mission outreach ourselves. We presented our plans to do a humanitarian effort we called Mission Masindi to our pastor and church authorities. We needed their blessing and prayer coverage, but we did not want them to support us financially. Our purpose was to set an example for others that one person really can make a difference in the world. We wanted to show that you don't have to be a big organization to affect positive change, and it doesn't take millions of dollars, either.

The average person in Uganda only makes $120 for a whole year. You can feed a starving person for a full year for less than seventy-five dollars. In other words, you can actually save someone's life for less than one hundred dollars. Are you listening? Do you understand you can actually prevent someone from starving to death?

If you don't trust charities, churches, or organizations to get your donations into the hands of the people who need it, then do it yourself. Please don't just sit back and do nothing while using the excuse that everyone and everything is corrupt. If, on the other hand, you don't donate to charities because you think your contribution is so small that it wouldn't do much good anyway, then please go back and read the previous paragraph again about the small cost to feed someone and save his or her life.

Time and time again I prayed, "God, I'll try to do whatever you want me to do, but please don't make me ask anyone for the money to do it." Melainie and I were determined to do what we could afford on our own, without asking anyone for additional funds. We set aside enough money for me to travel two or three times each year to Masindi. That only left me with small amounts of money to spend on the people when I got there.

I started by hand-carrying tools, clothes, food, and books into different villages in the Masindi District and gave them directly to the people myself. The cost to do this was less than we would spend on a two-week vacation for ourselves.

It was so easy to help people. One small bottle of aspirin relieved the pain and suffering of many people. What seemed like little, insignificant things to us were big things to them.

Packing for these trips was challenging. Traveling alone, I was restricted to two suitcases of a certain size and weight. That was the biggest problem with getting items into Uganda. I could pay for extra baggage, but the cost was astronomical. It was less expensive to purchase items in Uganda (if you could find those items) than to transport them from the United States.

It worked to my advantage when I took other passengers along with me, like my wife or my son. That way we could put all our personal needs in one suitcase, and I could take five other suitcases maxed out with all kinds of medicines, clothes, shoes, and tools.

Getting through customs with everything was never a problem. I never got stopped by the Ugandan custom officers for an inspection. Not one suitcase or package I took into Uganda in five years was ever inspected. I assure you it was not my good looks that got me through customs every time. It was God.

The only international airport in Uganda is in Entebbe. From there, I had to hire drivers and vehicles to transport me approximately 250 kilometers (155 miles) out to the Masindi District. I hired a Muslim man named Badru to guide, drive, and interpret for me. Before heading out into the country alone, we went directly to the United States Embassy and registered my plans and locations for tracking purposes in case we disappeared.

The first time I walked into the secured and heavily armed embassy, a lot of hustle and bustle was going on. Americans in Uganda were being bombed, and the U.S. called for an immediate helicopter evacuation of all U.S.

Do It Yourself

Peace Corp Personnel. This was not an encouraging way to get started.

They reviewed my travel plan and told me, "You should be all right. They are targeting groups of Americans, not individuals, so traveling alone, you should be alright." "*Should* be?" I thought. That wasn't exactly what I wanted to hear. The only warning they gave me was not to go north of Masindi. Just a two-hour drive north was the Sudan, and the Sudanese were infiltrating northern Uganda in what they called a holy war. It was impossible to travel north of Masindi, even in convoys.

The majority of roads in the Masindi District are narrow, one-lane, dirt surfaces with tall brush growing right up to the sides of your car. The brush is so high you can't see what is ahead of you or to the sides, and as the car kicks dust up you can't see what is behind you. You drive through a maze until you reach a clearing, which signals when you are approaching a village.

As we were arriving in the Katama Village one night after dark, a crowd of people started running alongside our car shouting "mzungu" and pointing at us. As we slowed down, the people pressed up against the car still shouting the word: *mzungu.*

It was pitch-black outside. There were only small cooking fires for light, so when I looked out the car windows, I couldn't see any of the faces in the crowd. When they started slapping their hands against the car, I got racked with fear, expecting to be dragged out of the car at any moment. Close to where we were, a family had been hacked apart with machetes just three days earlier and their body parts were strewn around in front of their home.

I was in a frenzy. I looked over at Badru and asked him, "What's wrong? Should we get out of here?" Badru smiled, giggled a little, and in his broken English said, "No, it's OK. They shout *mzungu* because you're here." With a great sigh of relief, I listened as Badru went on to explain that *mzungu* means "white pastor" in Swahili. They were happy and most excited that a mzungu had come to visit them.

Deciding what to take with me on these trips was difficult. They needed everything.

One time I packed a whole set of silverware. It was so heavy that I couldn't take many more items because I couldn't go over the weight limit. I decided to leave the silverware out.

Notice I said I decided? See how easy it is to forget to pray first and ask for guidance?

I repacked the suitcase to get more things in, but I was still bothered by the silverware. I kept thinking of how many families could share this silverware instead of eating with their fingers.

Back in the suitcase the silverware went. Hours later, the silverware came out again. I packed, unpacked, and repacked that silverware a dozen times. I couldn't decide whether to take it or not. Frustrated with myself, I threw the silverware in the suitcase at the last minute and said, "God, I don't know what to do here, but I have to get going."

When I arrived, I saw a boy in the Katama village who

I had prayed over for healing on a previous visit. The boy had recovered, so in gratitude their custom was for the family to feed me a meal. When I visited their home, I took advantage of the opportunity to get rid of that heavy silverware I had been toting around and presented it to Catherine, the boy's mother, as a gift.

When she unwrapped the package, she got a blank look on her face and stared at me. In astonishment she said, "God has answered my prayers. Two days ago I was in the market to buy spoons. I had spoons in my hands but I could not afford them, so I put them down. I kept going back to the spoons and picking them up and putting them down. I did this many times, until I finally had to return home sad that I would not have spoons to feed you."

She had been picking up and putting down the spoons in the market at the very same time I was putting the silverware in and out of my suitcase.

On one occasion, we spent a night in a mud hut near Murchison Falls, which is on the Victoria Nile River. These were the falls that actually dammed up in spots due to the massive number of dead bodies that were thrown into the river after an ethnic cleansing in the 1980s.

The hut was round, about nine feet in diameter. The walls were made of mud built to about four feet high, and there was an open space between the top of the walls and the thatched straw roof. The doorway was just an opening; there was no actual door. The inside furnishings consisted of a dirt floor and two wood platforms that were barely above the ground. You laid your sleeping bag on the platform, pulled a mosquito net down from the ceiling, and wrapped it around you to sleep. This was the typical home in Uganda. Comfy, huh?

The hut was so open to the elements that baboons, gorillas, and anything else could walk right in during the night. I had a roommate that night from Habitat for Humanity, a man named Alan, who was more accustomed to these conditions than I was.

Our only light came from our flashlights, and when you turned them off you couldn't see your hand in front of your face. Walking outside the hut at night was dangerous because hippopotami from the Nile graze on land. If you accidentally walk between mates or a mother and her calf in the dark, they will trample you to death.

That night a thrashing noise woke me up. It was obvious something was in the hut with us. I reached for my flashlight, and guess what? It rolled somewhere outside my mosquito net and I couldn't find it. I was trying to move stealthily so as not to make a sound that would alarm whatever was visiting us. When crunching noises began, I softly called out to Alan, but he didn't wake up. My heart was in my throat. Suddenly the noise stopped with one last, loud crunch.

I called out to Alan again, but to no avail. I assured myself that he was just sleeping and not a victim of that last crunch. The next day Alan was up first and standing over me saying good morning. I sat up and looked around the room expecting to see the whole placed trashed, but not a thing had been disturbed. I asked Alan if he heard anything during the night, and he replied, "No, I'm a very sound sleeper."

We crawled out of the hut and spoke to a Ugandan guide who was sleeping near us. I told him what I heard during the night, and he got a big smile on his face as he said, "Ah, so close. You're lucky to be alive. Hippos graze around huts. Many die when hippos crush mud walls."

Before long, our efforts with Mission Masindi grew into a ministry. I hired Pastor Rwomushana Kibuuka Robert to travel around to small villages and preach the gospel for us.

Our main goal was still to install a water well in the Katama village. It was in that village that I had helped build three nice brick homes with tin roofs and concrete floors with Habitat for Humanity. After that visit, three families had stable, durable homes to live in. However, I knew that their home was only helpful to them if they didn't die from drinking the water there.

I wanted to spare the people in Katama from the burden of traveling great distances twice a day to get a bucket of water and to save them from the illnesses of drinking from such heavily polluted water sources. The rivers and streams were loaded with run-off of natural jungle rot, plus animal urine and feces.

The cost to drill a well in Uganda could range anywhere from one to ten thousand dollars, depending on the location and geographical composition of the area. There were drilling companies we could hire in Uganda, but, boy, were they antiquated. Much time and money had to be invested just to get the equipment on site and then to keep that equipment working without daily mechanical failures.

Still, Melainie and I were determined to pay for this our own. We just casually told people what we hoped to do. Without asking anyone to donate anything, people started approaching us saying, "Hey, I heard you're putting a well in Africa. Can I help do that? Can I give you some money for that?" Others came to us and asked, "Are you still traveling to Africa? Can you use some extra clothes to take over there?" And others yet inquired, "Didn't you say you took books to Africa? I've got some old encyclopedias in my basement. Can you use those?"

With this kind of response and donations from people, it only took us a few months before we could afford to have a land survey done, hire a drilling company, and finish a well (called a borehole in Uganda) in the Katama Village.

Derek went to Uganda with me one time. He was fourteen, and his job was to help me deliver supplies to schools and survey potential well sites. His assistance qualified as one of the quarterly community service projects that were required by the private Christian high school he attended. It was a calm and productive trip, even though we narrowly missed an outbreak of the Ebola virus. The virus broke out in the area that we had just left, and people were dying there as we were on the plane flying home.

Melainie went with me one time, and it turned out to be one of the most dangerous trips. The Lord's Resistance

Army (LRA) was a band of ruthless rebels who would sweep through western Uganda and mutilate everyone in their path. They didn't want to kill; they specifically wanted to leave mutilated victims behind because that would create more horror and terror than death. When the LRA had gathered all the food and supplies they wanted, they retreated back into the Congo to hide until their next rampage.

With our work completed for that trip, Pastor Robert was escorting Melainie and me back to Entebbe through an alternate route in order to visit another site for a future well. Little did we know that the alternate road he took us on was the front line of the war with the LRA. Robert didn't tell us that before we got there because it was such common knowledge to him that he didn't think a thing of it. He also didn't think anything about it when our vehicle broke down. With our vehicle and engine dead in the middle of a dirt road, Robert told us he had to walk back to the nearest village to contact a relative and get us another ride. At that, he said to Melanie and I, "It's OK. You'll be fine." and walked away.

There we sat on the frontlines of a war—two white people with a suitcase full of money. In Ugandan currency, we were transporting about eight million dollars to a bank in Kampala.

Walking past us in both directions were unfriendly looking soldiers and civilians, all wielding razor sharp machetes. No one was smiling at us. We couldn't tell the civilians from the soldiers, much less the good guys from the bad guys.

My lightning-fast brain told me to get the money out of the car and hide it in the brush. I took off so fast Melainie didn't even know I had left the car. I had tried to go quickly, when I thought no one was watching me; I didn't think about Melainie not seeing me, either. As I came leaping back out of the brush, Melainie shouted, "Where have you been?" When I told her I went to hide the money, she shouted in a tone of voice I will never forget, "Hide the money? The heck with the money. Hide me!" It wasn't very long before Robert showed up in another four-wheel drive vehicle, and we left the scene in a big hurry.

Feet are the only means of transportation for most Ugandans. Vehicles of any kind were rare; everyone walked. After all the traveling we had done, it was divine providence that allowed us to break down only when we were close to one of Pastor Robert's relatives, much less a relative who happened to have a vehicle.

It was between my trips to Uganda that I went with that Flying Hospital team to Mexico. Before the staff elected me to manage the clinic, they heard I was trying to install a well in Africa. Since I had been a *700 Club* member for over twenty-five years, they interviewed me and wrote an article about my involvement with them in their CBN monthly newsletter, titled *Frontlines*.

They also suggested I meet with a woman who managed funds for Operation Blessing, just to let her know who I was and what I was doing in Africa. When I met with her, she was very kind and expressed her appreciation of my efforts and past support of the CBN organization, but she went on to inform me that they couldn't help me install a well in Africa. This information came as a surprise, since I had not asked for her help. However, I listened as she went on to explain that if we would consider installing multiple wells, the organization could match funds toward the cost of the projects. That, I could do.

Of all the contributions we received for Mission Masindi, I never had to ask anyone for anything. We surpassed our goals and completed our work in Uganda in just five short years. Here's the result of what two ordinary people (Melainie and I) did with God's help:

- We received unsolicited cash donations of $92,881, which converted to more than $162,000,000 in Ugandan money.

- We installed six wells, which provided water for over nine thousand people.

- We took the gospel to more than 13,500 people, gaining 784 new Christians and converts from Islam and tribal religions.

- We provided clothing and personal hygiene supplies to 2,100 people in thirteen villages.

- We delivered over four hundred books and encyclopedias to four schools.

- We built a large latrine and multi-shower facility for an orphanage of nine hundred children.

In others words, we made a difference. We changed their world, and because of it, a whole lot more people know God is real.

Chapter 25
A LOT MORE

AM I FINISHED? ARE THOSE ALL OF MY TESTIMOnies? Not by a long shot.

I could tell you how God answered a prayer for me by displaying a Bible verse on an electronic billboard, or how a devout Shiite Muslim sheik took me, a Christian, into his home and risked his life to shelter me in the dangerous West Bank of Egypt.

I could tell you about my eleven-year-old son, Derek, discerning an evil spirit in a Hindu temple by feeling pain every time he would walk in front of a specific demonic painting. Or, I could explain to you the circumstances when Derek and I saw a lost medical document rematerialize out of thin air.

These are still just the beginning.

By 2004, Melainie had been retired from Southwestern Bell for a few years and was serving as a director of volunteer services for the United Service Organization (USO), an organization that provides a variety of free services and support for our United States military forces.

Derek graduated from high school as a National Honor Society student and was attending the same junior college I went to.

As for me, I closed the toolboxes of Christian Works to take a job as a millwork sales specialist in my favorite "man's store," The Home Depot. The sales associates at The Home Depot soon became my new mission field. I was always looking for the slightest opportunity to share my belief in God with anyone I could get to listen.

I invited Tasha, a single woman from work, to join Melainie and me for church one Sunday. From our discussions, I thought she would be impressed with our praise and worship services in our non-denominational church. She enjoyed it very much, and then she invited us to return the favor and visit her church. I was happy to do that, but I didn't have a clue what God was setting me up for.

Tasha never let on that her church was so similar to ours. I don't know what I was expecting, but I sure didn't expect Melainie to get bowled over by the presence of God there. Melainie had found a new church home from the first day we walked in the door, but not me. Why would I want to leave the church where I received miraculous healings and got filled with the Holy Ghost? I wasn't interested in changing churches, but I was willing to visit there once in a while to appease my wife.

A LOT MORE

Well, it only took a couple more visits there before I was hooked. It was such a treat to find the same overflowing of the Holy Spirit in another church. It didn't seem to matter which church I was in; God was always there. I started having my own personal revival every Sunday we visited there. It was great, and Melainie was forever hinting that we should just move our membership. I was convinced. I wanted to do that, but it felt like I was doing something wrong to leave a church where God had blessed me so mightily.

Then I found out the church Tasha led us to, Twin Rivers Worship Center, was a denominational church, aligned with the Church of God. I, Mr. Anti-Establishment, was not inclined to align myself with a denomination after already persuading Melainie away from one, but all God had to do was remind me of my own words: "I'm a Christian, and that means I'm a member of all denominations or I'm a member of none." When faced with my own words, God showed me I already was a member of all denominations by being a part of the whole Christian body. Since God put arms, legs, feet, and hands on a human body, He must have put Baptists, Methodists, Catholics, and Lutherans on the Christian body, too.

That revelation allowed me to receive another level of freedom. I was freed from my hang-up with "labeling." I got the peace and assurance I needed from God that I wasn't doing anything wrong to change churches or join a denomination. I was just following Him. This was a set-up from God from the get-go. Melainie and I officially—and proudly—joined in membership with Twin Rivers.

We already knew several people at our new church, but by our own desire we stayed pretty much unknown in the congregation for quite a while. Melainie and I were taking that time to rest and prepare for what God had in store for us next.

Our pastor there was Dr. Bryan Cutshall, or "Pastor B" as we affectionately called him. Pastor B did a teaching encouraging us to speak up and be a witness for God. This teaching took several Sundays to complete. I was so moved by one of the services I sent him a copy of my testimony about my finger healing.

On October 30, 2005, Pastor B's message was titled "I Will Not Be Silent." Melainie and I attended the second service, and to do something different for a change, we sat over to the far right side of the sanctuary instead of where we normally sat. To be really radical, we buried ourselves deep in the middle of everyone instead of sitting in our usual end seats.

At one point in Pastor B's message, he was standing in the center of the pulpit facing the congregation and began by saying, "Now in your prosperity..." He paused, turned quickly, and walked directly toward me, saying sharply, "Roy," before he walked back to the center and continued with, "...is the time. Don't remain silent."

Pastor B looked as surprised by having called out my name as I was to hear it. At that time, he and I had not personally met. He couldn't have called me by name if I had walked up to him. I knew, from that moment on, I couldn't remain silent any longer. I had refrained from telling some of my testimonies over the years because I didn't want people to think I was crazy. Well, I'm not crazy, but it is time I speak up so my testimonies can reveal to you, and others, that God is real.

Chapter 26
YOUR TURN

WHEN I REFLECT BACK OVER WHAT I HAVE written in this book, I can't help but wonder why God doesn't just fix all the problems in the world right now. Why would God miraculously heal my stomach and my finger, but let me struggle with neck pains, common colds, and headaches? Why is it that when I pray for an illness one day, it goes away immediately, and when I pray for that very same illness another time, it lingers on and even gets worse before it gets better?

The testimonies that I have collected over the years have answered these questions for me. God actually did all the things I have written in this book. I know He is capable to do those things, so I am OK when He doesn't respond as I wish He would. In other words, I have seen what God can do, so I can accept what He doesn't do. It's not that God is random, inconsistent, or not in control. It is that only He knows what to do and when to do it.

Do all my testimonies mean I'm more special to God than you are? Nope. Then why did God allow me to experience all these things? Maybe because I just plain believed in Him, or maybe because I tried to live a godly life. Notice I said "tried" to live a godly life. I didn't say I succeeded, but I believe God will bless us just for trying.

What is a godly life? That brings us back to the most volatile word of all times: *Jesus*. Jesus set the standards for what a godly life is, and Jesus explained how a person gets to spend eternity in the presence of God.

I don't just think God is the God of the Christian faith (and not Allah, Shiva, or Buddha) because I grew up in America and that is what I was taught. No, I've studied the Koran to learn what Muslims believe, and I've studied the gods of Hinduism and Buddhism and heard their persuasive arguments to support their beliefs. What makes me so sure I know the real God is that I have had personal experiences with Him that have convinced me that He is who the Bible says He is.

Still, whether you believe in God or not, it doesn't change the fact that you exist only because God is real. Your parents didn't create you, they just got the privilege to deliver you. It took God and only God to create you. As long as you are on this Earth, you will never be able to understand all the things of God.

Quit trying to reason or explain things away. Forget about scientific theories and political correctness. Stop worrying about what other people will think of you and teach your children that God is real. Get rid of your sins and live a godly life. You can't keep saying to yourself, "Someday

God will prove to me beyond any doubt that He is real," because someday may never come. You or I might die in the next second, so you have to believe and live like God is real now. You are going to spend eternity somewhere, either with God or without Him. There is nothing in-between.

I believed God was real just because Pop said so. And that simple belief started a lifetime of supernatural events for me. So, if Pop's words were good enough for me, then my testimonies should be good enough for you. Acknowledge God's supernatural power and go tell others, "God is real!"

ABOUT THE AUTHOR

To invite Roy Davidson to speak at your church or organization, contact him by E-mail at redav50@aol.com.

You may view photos of the author's missionary experiences and watch a video reenactment of his miraculous healing as it was televised on The 700 Club *at his Web site:*

www.roy-davidson.com

Portions of the proceeds from this book will be donated to organizations that provide aid to people who are suffering and in need. By purchasing this book you are making a contribution to others less fortunate than yourself.